THE VOICE IN THE WIND

UNDERSTANDING GOD'S PARTNERSHIP WITH US

David L. Ramer

Sapphire 777, LLC
Heathrow, FL

Copyright © 2023 by David L. Ramer

The Voice in the Wind

All rights reserved. This book was published by the author, David L. Ramer. No part of this book may be reproduced in any form by any means without the express written permission of the author. This includes reprints, excerpts, photocopying, recording, or any future means of reproducing text.

Published in the United States.

Unless otherwise identified, Scripture quotations are taken from the New King James Version

Scripture quotations taken from the New American Standard Bible® (NASB),

Copyright © 1960, 1962, 1963, 1968, 1971, 1972, 1973,

1975, 1977, 1995 by The Lockman Foundation

Scripture quotations marked "AMP" are taken from the Amplified® Bible, Copyright © 1954, 1958, 1962, 1964, 1965, 1987 by The Lockman Foundation.

Scripture quotations are from the ESV® Bible (The Holy Bible, English Standard Version®), copyright © 2001 by Crossway Bibles, a publishing ministry of Good News Publishers. Used by

permission. All rights reserved.

Scripture quotations marked TPT are from The Passion Translation®. Copyright © 2017, 2018, 2020 by Passion & Fire Ministries, Inc. Used by permission. All rights reserved. ThePassionTranslation.com.

Aramaic Bible in Plain English. The text is published by the British and Foreign Bible Society in 1905. Public Domain.

Any scriptures from the 1898 Young's Literal Translation of The Holy Bible by J.N. Young, (Author of the Young's Analytical Concordance), public domain.

Any scriptures from the JPS Tanakh is published in 1917, public domain.

Scripture quotations marked (NIV) are taken from the Holy Bible, New International Version®, NIV®. Copyright © 1973, 1978, 1984, 2011 by Biblica, Inc.™ Used by permission of Zondervan.

Scripture taken from the Holy Bible: International Standard Version® Release 2.0. Copyright © 1996-2013 by the ISV Foundation. Used by permission of Davidson Press.

The Holy Bible, Berean Study Bible, BSB Copyright ©2016, 2020 by Bible Hub. Used by permission. All Rights Reserved Worldwide.

Scripture quotations marked CSB have been taken from the Christian Standard Bible ®, Copyright © 2017 by Holman Bible Publishers. Used by permission. Christians Standard Bible ® and CSB®.

Editing by: Marcia Zimmermann, Beverly Zimmerman

Cover design: Rick Schroeppel

Front cover image: Marguerite Anderson - https://1-marguerite-anderson.pixels.com

Copyright ©, used with expressed written permission by the artist.

Printed in United States of America

First Edition

ISBN: 979-8-218-14870-6

To William

Someday, when the Lord sits me down to have a talk about all this,

I'm going to remind Him that it was you who started it.

Foreword

I know David as a pastor, with a prophetic edge, who is also gifted as an artist, who brilliantly portrays his artistic abilities in the most unique and colorful ways. I believe his pieces of art are destined to become a global expression of the life of God in him. David lives with a determination to reach his greater potential in the kingdom of God. And now his new book, "The Voice in the Wind," is yet another example of his gifts and abilities to express the revelation of the knowledge of God.

We are living in a time when the voice of God is essential to advancing the Ecclesia, the kingdom of God on Earth. God's people are continuing to exercise their ability as supernatural beings. What was once perceived as spiritual limitations are now being overrun by the increasing glory of heaven. As a prophetic people in God's kingdom, we are no longer just predicting future outcomes but creating them. The body of Christ is maturing into the revelation of sonship, thus exhibiting the authority of God in ways most never imagined. Even the laws of physics are beginning to bow to the kingdom authority of God in his people. What was once considered impossibilities are now giving way to "all things are possible for those who believe."

David's book opens new pathways and doors of unlimited revelation. His writings are pointed toward the seekers of God who have a desire to gain access to the unlimited divine nature in Christ. Those who were once waiting for God to do something are becoming more aware that God has been waiting for them do something; releasing the kingdom of heaven on Earth. "This treasure that is in earthen vessels" is becoming a visual reality for the whole world to recognize the unstoppable force of heaven. "The Voice in the Wind" that David Ramer so brilliantly describes in this book is literally accelerating across the earth at a category 10. Everything in its path is subject to the force of God's love and glory, in the end, nothing will escape its eternal intent.

In the book of Genesis, we read where Adam and Eve heard the movement of God in the wind, this is the "Ruach" of God's voice. The sound and movement of God was undoubtedly a daily experience in their lives. After sin entered the world, the voice of God eventually became faint. Only those who were close to God could still hear his voice.

Under this new covenant relationship in Christ, he has given us the Holy Spirit. We are now privileged to not only feel and hear the wind of God's voice, but to become the breath and life of God on the earth. In the spirit, there are endless jet streams of revelation flowing from the heart of God. As you read this book, you will be impacted by these same intense currents of kingdom revelation, all of which, will propel you closer towards your destiny in God.

Greater than any other time before, the wind of God is beginning to blow upon the body of Christ. This same wind is breaking down the strongholds of human tradition and doctrine. As a result, the voice of God will be heard throughout the world and the age of reformation and restoration will be known. Samuel the prophet spoke this word, *"He flew swiftly on his winged creature; he traveled on the wings of the wind."* He then declared, *"The Lord thundered from the sky and the voice of the almighty God was heard."* (2 Samuel 22:11&14) I have no doubt, as you read this book you will be winged with the wind of the Spirit and be lifted up into the voice of God.

Michael A Danforth - Danforth Ministries
Mountain Top International

Endorsements

Hang on to your seat! David's new book is jammed packed with anointed revelation and has a depth to it that is clear from the first pages. It has the flavor of a well-aged, full-bodied wine. The book begins by introducing the voice of God as the very breath of God and then proceeds to activate that in our lives through our identity as sons and daughters of God. This work was clearly not written lightly and was developed over time. The book then circles back and develops how to engage things in the physical, soul, and spirit realms. So deep! It will bless everyone who reads it, an education for Body of Christ. An apostolic and prophetic declaration to the heavenly realms. Congratulations, David.

Daniel Zelli – International speaker, Prophetic Minister

In this book, David states "believers often try to hear God speak with their natural mind, but God speaks spirit to spirit." I agree. In my experience, God speaks to us on many levels, whilst reading the Word or through dreams, visions, or even a natural sign that appears before us randomly in our daily life. Sometimes this can be hard to discern while living in the natural with all the surrounding noise and activities. If you desire a deeper understanding in hearing the voice of God, *The Voice in the Wind* will activate revelatory keys on hearing God's voice to be led by the spirit. Congratulations, David, for your obedience in writing this amazing manuscript.

Adam Thompson – Author, International Prophetic Minister

I've had the privilege of knowing and working in ministry with David Ramer over the past 20 years. More importantly, he is a friend. He understands what it takes to stay grounded in both his spirituality and his humanity as a prophetic voice for this generation. David possesses a deep gentleness and is unapologetic about what the Lord says and does. The voice of God is as multifaceted as God is, thus the need for authentic prophetic seers and ministers who correctly discern His voice. *The Voice in the Wind* is an important book because it displays the heart of God in empowering His people to be co-creators with Him. David's teaching gift opens a revelatory portal for others to follow into the unseen realm. He demystifies interpreting the voice on the journey and inspires us to be normal people who hear and walk with a supernatural God.

Dr. Barbie Breathitt – Author, Speaker, Breath of the Spirit Ministries

My friend David Ramer's book "The Voice in the Wind" is a beautiful gift to the body of Christ. David has captured the beauty of the voice of the Lord in these pages. As I read through this incredible book, I could feel the deep woo of His heart, into deeper encounter with His voice and deeper understanding and revelation of how He speaks. The breath of God is heavily upon this book and the Lord's rich wisdom contained in these chapters will equip you, awaken you and encourage you. I highly recommend this incredibly powerful book to you, it will mark your life.

Lana Vawser – Author, Prophetic Voice, International Speaker

I'm convinced we all have so much to learn about the Holy Spirit. It's as if the last 2000 years of knowing the Spirit's presence in our lives has just been the preamble to something far more powerful and life-altering. That's what makes this book so important. We need every resource we can get our hands on that can testify to the Spirit's presence in our lives, help us find an even deeper connection, and prepare us for even more Holy Spirit interaction. David, and his wife, Ronda, have been walking this out for decades both in their ministry and mission work all over the world. The thoughts, testimony, and instructions herein are born out of a life of following the Spirit's lead and believing for even greater things. My time spent around them, and reading this book, has been the greatest encouragement. *The Voice of the Wind* is just the book needed today as we open ourselves to all of the Holy Spirit's power and intentions in our lives.

Christopher Carter – Author, Physicist, Discover the Heavens Ministries

I am happy to endorse Pastor David's book, *The Voice in the Wind*. It's a must read and a very powerful book for the days we live in. Pastor David is a gifted man of God whom God has given revelation and an end time vision for the Church. This book will open your prophetic ear to hear what the Spirit is saying to the Church today. I have known Pastor David for many years and he has been very faithful in the work of God and remains very encouraging to everyone he meets. Always abounding in love for God and His work, he tirelessly helps people everywhere. He has been a personal encouragement to my life and ministry as well. I know this book will be a blessing to many.

Prophetess Glenda Jackson

Our words are like keys in the realm of the Spirit, unlocking and thus opening the doors God leads us to enter. We do this in partnership with him. See, we do not speak on our own accord or from our own ambition, but as servants of God who speak what is seen and heard in secret. God stretched forth his hand to touch the mouth of his young prophet, Jeremiah saying, "behold, I have put my words in your mouth…" Jeremiah 1:9. *"When your words agree with God, they become one with God."* A quote from *The Voice in the Wind* by my friend, David Ramer. We have boldness in our words when they are in sync with God's heart, will, and word. With this being said, I want to heartily endorse this incredible book. *The Voice in the Wind* will help you recognize that God is always speaking and that he wants his voice to thunder through his sons to release change and creative power on earth. I have known Pastor David and his wife, Ronda for 10 years and ministered at their church many times. I can attest to his true heart for the Lord and know that this book you hold in your hands was birthed from intimate time inclining the ear to hear what the Holy Spirit is saying to this generation. You will be thankful you read this gem of a book!

Apostle Charlie Shamp – Destiny Encounters International, Author; Angels, Transfigured, Altars, Mystical Prayer

Dedication

Dedicated to my loving wife, Ronda

"A wife of noble character, who can find?
She is worth far more then rubies." (Proverbs 31:10)

It is only fitting that I dedicate this book to my wife, Ronda, who has been a great wife, business partner, co-pastor and my greatest encourager in the most difficult of times. It was she who encouraged me to pursue writing and the development of my skill. She reminded me of the prophetic words spoken over me for many years before I picked up a pen or clicked the first keystroke to record the wonderful things God speaks.

She is recognized among her peers as an advanced prophetic seer, teacher and dream interpreter. Much like Daniel in the Bible, she remains fully committed to solving difficult sayings and the mysteries of how God speaks. On several occasions, Ronda's gift and anointing have provided an ability to hear the voice in the wind, saving many people's lives from much grief and difficulty. By receiving revelation from heaven, giving them understanding, hope, and spiritual warnings, not only is she an asset to the kingdom of God but to me personally. I could not do this without her.

Acknowledgements

I am grateful to God, who, through the Holy Spirit, brought me out of the spiritual darkness and dead works of religion into His glorious light and hope. I am grateful for the voice of Holy Spirit in the wind that makes all things possible.

A special acknowledgment to Apostle William D. Hinn, Ph D. who opened the doors of revelation and understanding into the depth of God's original creation, intent and design. You introduced me to a new world in the depth of scriptures regarding our true identity, calling, and purpose as sons. Together, we were forerunners in this journey before many accepted, believed, and hungered for more of the deep things of the spirit.

I want to acknowledge my wife, Ronda, who was patient as I travailed many hours over clarity, accuracy, and important details. I am grateful that you have joined me on this journey of discovery and tolerated the very late hours and schedule. Your sharp eye and perception of things in the spirit helped keep things on track.

I give special thanks to the late John Paul Jackson, who taught and modeled the importance of character first, then many other things regarding seeing in the spirit. John Paul, you have influenced my life in many positive ways without knowing it. You added an important layer of impartation and understanding of the awe of God. Journaling dreams and interpretation were foundational stones to discerning the voice in the wind. I appreciate the impartation.

A special thanks also to the editor, writer, and director of art for Streams Ministries, the late Carolyn Blunk, who set me up to win. Carolyn was more convinced of my writing abilities than I was and gave me my first chance to get published. Your red pen markings all over my pages showed me I still had a long way to go, but you never gave correction without giving ideas how to improve.

I want to thank Terry Bennett as a prophetic seer, one of the first to see the books in advance and encourage me to begin the writing process.

Thanks to Papa Jack Taylor, who encouragingly said, *"Words are like a vapor. If you don't write them down, they will disappear like smoke."*

Thanks to Jamie Galloway, who saw at least five books in me and prophesied that one or two may be novels. It was not long afterward, while on a trip to India, upon leaving the Bangalore International Airport, I heard the voice in the wind whisper a title in my ear, "The Barking Dogs of Bangalore." It prompted my first novel, which has only one chapter to date. I must get back to that.

Thanks to Pastor Rick Penny, who dared to tell his dream of me writing a book on covenant that became a Christian classic and went worldwide. I haven't written that one yet, but I love you for having the courage to share the dream with me. Sometime later I had a visitation to the library in heaven, where I was lifted to a top shelf in that very large room. A book with a golden cover and red letters floated out of a long line of books so that I could read the title, *The Blood of the Lamb.* I am sure that is the one on covenant. I just need to go back and read the content, but I know it's already in me.

Prophetess Glenda Jackson, you not only brought angels into the house when you lived with us, but you left a residue of the heavenly realm for encounters and healing. Since then, others have been healed and have received divine spiritual counsel, encounters and revelation while sleeping in those rooms. We honor the legacy and spiritual inheritance from your Great Aunt Maria Woodworth-Etter, seeing the past, present and future. You have been gracious in sowing many hours of your time in prayer, instruction, and counsel. You saw the books and prophesied them into existence. We are grateful for your encouragement to keep seeing into the eternal realm and sharing it with us.

Special thanks to my friend Christopher Carter, a spiritual physicist, who dares to stretch the boundaries of spiritual discovery beyond the norm. In your love for God and science, you create a sensible approach to accessing the heavenly realm and mysteries of God that has encouraged many of us to walk into the mysteries beyond our comfort zone. You opened many doors to gaze upon the beauty of God. We all needed that.

A special thanks to my father-in-law, Richard J Smith Sr., a master gardener who has taught me how to care for all things growing. He has modeled well the art of patience from planting a seed, pruning, and weeding unto reaping a harvest. Under his direction, I discovered the necessity of having a well-executed plan for best results. Writing a book is much like gardening. Behind the scenes, you must get into hard areas, prune and weed some ideas, while keeping the most eloquent of words for the beauty and aroma of the final bouquet for the desired result.

Finally, I'd like to thank Don Milam, a truly professional editor, writer, and director, for helping those taking their first steps in the world of getting published. Without you, none of this would have come to pass. Thank you for your generosity and care in handling the manuscript with love, along with adding your creative touch. You know what it takes to get it done. Thanks for your fatherly role in having the patience and sharing your expertise with the next generation of writers, giving us the possibility of leaving a legacy for future generations.

Contents

Foreword

Endorsements

Dedication

Acknowledgements

   1. From the Beginning... 1

   2. Sound of The Wind... 9

   3. Our Reformed DNA... 25

   4. Force Particles 37

   5. Valley of Dead Bones... 47

   6. Co-Creators... 57

   7. God and Time 73

   8. God's Diverse Languages 89

   9. Truth vs. Facts... 99

   10. Between Heaven & Earth.. 109

   11. The Voice of Many Waters 123

   12. Spirit vs. Soul.. 131

Endnotes

About the Author

CHAPTER ONE

From the Beginning

L ong before God spoke any words to man, He breathed, and things came into existence. The first thing the Bible tells us is that God is a creator. "In the beginning God created the heavens and the earth." (Gen. 1:1) God breathed a desired result and things materialized into existence that were not there before, beginning with the universe itself. Creation is solely an act of God. It is not an accident, a mistake, or the product of an inferior deity, but the self-expression of God. Genesis continues this discourse, emphasizing the materiality of the world. "The earth was a formless void and darkness covered the face of the deep, while a wind from God swept over the face of the waters." (Gen. 1:2) It was this phrase that caught my attention and held me captive to write this book. The wind of God hovered over the matter of creation. Does this wind have a sound? Is it a groaning much like speech but without words? That is what we are about to explore.

The embryonic creation, though still "formless," has the material dimensions of space ("the deep") and matter ("waters"), and God is fully engaged with this materiality ("a wind from God swept over the face of the waters"). In Genesis there is no sharp distinction between the material and the spiritual. The ruah of God in Genesis 1:2 is simultaneously "breath," "wind," and "spirit." Likewise, "the heavens and the earth" (Gen. 1:1; 2:1) are not two separate realms, but a Hebrew figure of speech meaning "the universe" in the same way that the English phrase "kith and kin" means "relatives."

Breathing is a very powerful biblical image. In Genesis, God creates humanity from the clay of the earth, yet the human being is merely a lifeless work of clay pottery until God breathes into the nostrils of the human. It is that first breath that gives us life. Aside from the physical birth of life through breath is the even greater significance that the breath comes straight from God. The Bible could have said that God had the winds of the earth or some other entity fill our lungs. Yet the scripture is very specific. God did it directly and personally.

The emphasis of Genesis 1 is on the creative power of God's Word being sufficiently great to produce the physical universe in accordance with God's perfect will. To reflect the greatness of God's powerful ability to produce all that He desires, God is referred to throughout all of chapter one as that which He is: God.

The Breath of the Soul

What makes man a living being then, is the breath of God in his soul. Genesis 2:7 tells us that man became a living soul (KJV). The word soul in Hebrew is 'nephesh,' meaning an animated breathing, conscious and living being. Man did not become a living soul until God breathed life into him. As a physical, rationale and spiritual being, man is unique among all living things upon the earth. The "breath of life" is the life and power of God, given to man to animate him.

To create life, you first must be a life source yourself. In effect, the life of man is not sustained by his organs, his heart, kidneys, or lungs. It is not even sustained by his brain. The brain is an organ in your head transmitting electrical impulses. Brain cells function using rapid electrical impulses, a process that underlies our thoughts, behavior, and perception of the world. The brain, the soul and the spirit are all different things. Then, to make it even more complex, there is the spirit of the mind which Paul talks about in Ephesians 4:23, *"and be renewed in the spirit of your mind."* It refers to the inner man, the very deepest part of who we are that determines how we think and what we do. This is our heart of hearts, the very deepest part of who we really are at our core. All the organs and functions of the body are dependent on the breath of God in man's soul. His soul is the seat of the mind, will, emotions, and nature. The soul is the spiritual nature of humankind, whereas, the mind is man's faculty of thinking, reasoning, and applying knowledge. Spirit is eternal, it doesn't depend on anything except from where it came, the spirit of God.

The Environment of Man

God created everything to exist and thrive in certain conditions or environments. The birds of the air need the skies and the air to fly. The fish of the sea need the oceans, lakes, rivers, and water to sustain their life and reproduction. What then is the condition or environment that man needs to truly thrive and be alive? I don't mean how to survive with food and water. As a living soul, man lives in the environment of his mind. As a soul, living in a body, man is the only created being that does not have to live in his localized body. Meaning, his body only identifies his location - not his life. Therefore, the life of God is in your soul. God made man a living soul, the seat of the mind, will and emotions. As an example, amongst the many joyful days I sat writing the chapters of this book, there were times I felt very unsettled. My body was sitting in front of my computer, but my mind was always somewhere else searching and listening. It was my spirit searching and discerning. These two, are closely related. Discernment is the skill of understanding and applying God's Word with the purpose of separating truth from error and right from wrong. When we practice discernment, we are applying the truths of the Bible to our lives. It is your spirit that drives the searching.

Our world is full of deep things. For example, the formation of rain is a complex and intricate phenomenon. Seasonal changes are deep things. The complex physical laws that govern our universe are deep things that scientists continue to investigate. There are deep things in the spiritual or religious realms as well. In the Christian faith, for example, the incarnation, atonement, and redemption are deep things. Even the Bible admits that spiritual matters are so deep that they can only be "spiritually discerned."

God's Search Engine

I like using Google as a search engine when shopping online, researching, or exploring a subject. But the most significant search engine in the universe is the Holy Spirit because the Spirit searches the mind of God and seeks out wisdom. His thoughts were absorbed with you for billions of years in past eternity. You are not a disappointment to Him. Our concept of the Father's loving heart must be clear before we can represent him properly. I Corinthians 2:9-10 says, *"Eye has not seen, nor ear heard, nor have entered into the heart of man the things which God has prepared for those who love Him. But God has revealed them to us through His Spirit. For the Spirit searches all things, yes, the deep things of God."*

When you go deep into the spirit, you ascend into the realm of the spirit and search out things. When I find my spirit stirred, I try to hear that whisper of the voice in the wind. Scripture states we've been translated out of darkness into the Kingdom of God's dear son. Locally your body can be in one place, but your mind can be elsewhere. Which means God has given the ability for our soul - as a living being - to transcend out of a localized arena into the unlimited realm of the spirit or God's mind.

Apart from God There is No Life

God's order for man is to function as the dwelling place of God. Otherwise he is not really a man. It stands to reason then, if a man is not the dwelling place of God, he's not yet a man. He is of the beastly realm, unbelieving, natural in thinking, "non-spiritual" as some translations put it. He might be human, he may look like a man, but he's not complete. He's not exactly working right. He needs a tune-up and some additional parts to make him complete. Man lives in the environment of his own mind - for better or worse. Proverbs 23:7, *"For as a man thinks in his heart, soul, mind so is he."* Meaning, how you reason in your own soul – you are.

The spiritual realm operates in a bandwidth we cannot see. I believe Adam could see it in his perfected state, and that God intends us to see it now. Every life-giving word God speaks to us has the potential to be a stroke of a paintbrush creating a doorway into a supernatural reality for us to walk into. The Father takes His paintbrush, if you will, and paints a picture that creates a doorway for us to enter the supernatural realm. The Father's invitation into the covenant that He's made with us in written form, can only be experienced by entering in to it. Entering covenantal agreements were a major part of what it meant to live in the ancient Near East. God partnered with humans through a structure they already understood. The earliest covenant recorded is when God invites Adam and Eve to be priest kings and represent His generous rule on Earth. They could enjoy and reproduce blessings of eternal life if they continued to trust and partner with Him.

The purpose of civil government is to bring order through common laws so that people can live in a place of safety, security, blessing and empowerment. God's kingdom is the blessing that empowers us to be fruitful, to multiply, to fill the earth. It allows us to subdue all obstacles and to rule with governmental authority – and then to expand that out into the rest of the solar system, galaxy, universe, dimensions and beyond. Isaiah 9 tells us there is no end to the increase of His government and of peace. One glance at the world around us confirms it is in chaos. The world is in a state of decay, and once decay begins, you cannot stop it, only slow it down. The process of decay can only be stopped by replacing it with a superior process. Enter the sons of the Kingdom, the Body of Christ that establishes His government here on earth. (Matthew 6:10) Every day they are growing in power and authority through intimacy with Christ Himself. There are many ways that we look for evidence of God's Spirit working and all of them are viable and wonderful. Yet in the desire to see God's spiritual power in bold manifestations, let us not forget the simple, subtle, and profound way we can have the Spirit present in every minute—literally every breath.

Superiority of the Spirit Realm

Job, upon spending much time with God, entered the secret place, a place of seeing in the spirit realm. Visions began to flow. Job was awakened in the spirit realm to something new happening. He was awakened to the point that his physical body responded by his hair standing up, his body shook, and his bones began trembling. Notice, Job did not see anything at first. He did not see a clear image of the form of the Holy Spirit. Rather, it was a mystical experience that lead to revelation. It's a mistake to think that instant clarity will always be given when coming across the things of the Spirit. The biblical model for encountering mystical things is quite clear: additional revelation is needed to decipher that which was shown. Many enigmas exist in the spirit; however, the Holy Spirit is our guide to solve the riddles and make clear what once was murky.

The spirit realm is superior to the natural realm we presently see. The seen realm was created from and by the unseen realm. By faith we understand that the worlds were framed by the Word of God, so that the things which are seen were not made of things which are visible. (Hebrews 11:3) It is a little strange to think of something solid and seen being created out of something unseen. But unseen does not mean un-real. Before you experience the unseen realm, it can be difficult to firmly grasp that reality. After you have seen and/or experienced the unseen realm you get it completely. We need to become aware that we do live in both realms. Whether we are cognizant of it or not, it is a reality.

The Bible says that we are already seated in Heavenly places in Christ. (Ephesians 2:6) We must understand these scriptures in a different way. We need to understand them in a way that acknowledges supernatural things as being supernatural. The spirit realm is more solid than this physical realm because the physical realm is temporal, fleeting, and in decay. The things of this earth were created from sources originating in the spirit realm. Therefore, the created is subject to the creator, making that the superior realm. God is not of this earth, a place where there is death, disease, and imperfection. His realm is supernatural. Our realm is terrestrial. The earthly space He occupies is made sacred and otherworldly by His presence. The space we occupy is ordinary. God is the polar opposite of ordinary. It's time we look at ourselves through supernatural eyes. You are a child of God, fit for sacred space, not because of what you do or don't do, but because you are in Christ, adopted by God. You've been extracted from the realm of darkness and "transferred to the kingdom of his beloved Son."

Life over Death

At the point of death, the same breath God gave us returns to Him. (Ecclesiastes 12:7) As with our birth, the presence of breath is not only equated with biological life, but that life is clearly attributed to the Author of Life, our sovereign creator God. We often refer to death as though it snuffs out life. I'd like to turn that around and say that with every God-given breath you take, you defeat death one breath at a time. Death comes to the physical body only after the breath of God leaves the body, making the breath of life greater than death. Therefore, death only fills the vacuum where there is no life as a natural occurrence.

Breath in the Bible is far more than the physical exchange of air in and out of the lungs. It is one of the most profound symbols in scripture. Breath in both the New Testament Greek and the Old Testament Hebrew is equated with God's Spirit. Think about it. When the Bible talks about filling our lungs with the breath of God or that breath that gives us our life, departing and returning to God, it is not making analytical notations about air. That Biblical breath is the Holy Spirit living in us.

How often do we hear the wind? Sometimes we cannot ignore the wind, especially as it shakes and rumbles along the walls and rooftop of this building as we worship, but often the wind is making a soft and gentle noise that we generally do not hear. It is by stopping and listening to the wind that we are being attentive to the Holy Spirit. I believe this is what the contemplative, Henri Nouwen had in mind when he suggested that we listen to the inner voice of Love. He wrote, "Have you ever tried to spend a whole hour doing nothing but listening to the voice that dwells deep in your heart? It is not easy to enter into the silence and reach beyond the many boisterous and demanding voices of our world and to discover there the small intimate voice saying: "You are my Beloved Child, on you my favor rests." Still, if we dare to embrace our solitude and befriend our silence, we will come to know that voice." Blaise Pascal said, "All of humanity's problems stem from our inability to sit quietly in a room."[i]

Have you ever tried to spend a whole hour doing nothing but listening to the voice that dwells deep in your heart? … It is not easy to enter the silence and reach beyond the many boisterous and demanding voices of our world and to discover there the small intimate voice saying: "You are my Beloved Child, on you my favor rests." Still, if we dare to embrace our solitude and befriend our silence, we will come to know that voice.

The best part is, even when we are not aware of it, that powerful Spirit fills our lives in ways we may never fully know or appreciate. One does not have to be a champion breather to have breath. Neither does one have to be a champion Christian to have God's Spirit flowing within. Furthermore, when we are least able to take the time to think of God and His presence, just like breathing, God is still right there. If that is reality when we are not thinking about it, imagine the power when we take the time to be deliberate and really give God's Holy Spirit some serious thought! Breathe. Breathe deep. Fill your lungs with the breath that flows from the One who created you and called you Good. It's worth every breath you take!

CHAPTER TWO

Sound of The Wind

Each day is a gift and comes with the capacity of a new beginning. This gift includes a mixture of sounds on an autumn day, the crunching leaves, the crackling sound of firewood screaming up the chimney and roaring waterfalls crashing against the rocks below, the high-pitched sound of a leaf blower, and the cries of geese flying south, the pitter-patter of rain on the rooftop, and in the evening the sublime harmonies of Mozart reaching their crescendo. And there is the whisper of a grandchild sharing a secret, the blare of a firetruck's siren entering the intersection, the soothing melody of your favorite song on the radio.

Jesus knew understanding spiritual truths is not easy for the natural man. So, to make things clearer, He used this illustration about the wind; *"The wind blows where it wants to, and you hear the sound of it, but you do not know where it comes from and where it is going. So it is with everyone who has been born from the spirit"* (John 3:8). Nicodemus could hear, feel, and see the effects of the wind, but he could not understand its source or its destination. Yet, the reality of the wind was beyond question. For him to understand the spiritual parallels of wind would present more challenging questions. Jesus invited Nicodemus into a deeper kind of listening. In the Synoptic Gospels (Matthew, Mark, and Luke) Jesus often says, *"Whoever has ears, let them hear!"* In John, Jesus is saying the same thing here in a more subtle and poetic way. Through concentrated listening, we will learn about the Spirit of God. The English poet William Wordsworth said, *"One impulse from a vernal wood can teach you more of man, of moral evil and of good, than all the sages can."* Wordsworth and Jesus invite us to appreciate the gift of hearing by listening to the wind.

One could say that appearing like the wind is what the prophet Elijah did. There is no genealogy for Elijah. He just appears. Where did that man come from? Where did that man go? He came and prophesied and spoke words that were hated. He fled so quick, he could not be caught. One could even say that Elijah was caught up on angel's wings. You cannot see wind, just the effects it has on things.

When you are in the middle of a windstorm, the sound seems to be coming at you from all directions, and when you're born of the Spirit, you do not typically see the spirit, just the effects it has. Those that are born of the spirit are like the wind of God, who come with purpose to deliver a message. God calls everyone to experience the divine wind, also known as the ancient ruah. The Hebrew word, ruah translates as both wind and Spirit that moved over the primordial waters during creation. God's breath of life—eternal, present in creation, untamed—sends us today to proclaim divine justice and mercy for all. As we respond to God's invitation to first hear and then proclaim the voice in the wind, we are reminded, like Nicodemus, that we never know for sure what lies ahead of us. The Spirit, like the wind, blows freely where it pleases, and we can't control it.

The Rushing Wind

It is interesting that Luke does not say in Acts 2 that a wind actually blew. He writes that the sound of a mighty, rushing wind came. Whatever the case, it had a hurricane-like sound that was understood or perceived to be coming from heaven. It filled the whole house where they were sitting. Why does he mention them sitting? Why were they not standing around and fellowshipping with one another? The "house" mentioned here is most likely the Temple. They were sitting because it was a holy day, and they were having a service.

Note too that the sound filled only the house, not the whole city, denoting relationship. Even if we allow that some of the sound was heard in the area around the house, Luke specifically contains the sound to the general area where the house was. We know that some outside (at least outside of the room the disciples were in) heard it, because they were attracted by the fact that the sound was emanating from the place where the disciples were sitting and having a meeting. So, these other people, a few thousand of them (Acts 2:41), began gathering in the general area, lending more credence to the probability that the "house" was the Temple. When the Holy Spirit was given, it came much like a mighty rushing wind. It had no shape at all and no life, but it appeared as the power the Father and the Son used to carry out their purposes in this creation. In this case it was specifically designated to believers in the house. This power not only filled the people, but it also filled the house. In this way, it was directed indiscriminately.

The wind of the Spirit has a unique feel and different work apart from the wind of the earth. Just as man cannot restrain the power of the wind, neither can he restrain the power of God. Although we cannot see the wind, we see its changing effects on the earth. We rarely see the Holy Spirit, but commonly see the changing effects He has in the lives of people who yield to Him. What a magnificent change the wind of the Holy Spirit brings. We can't really comprehend it, there are no words to adequately explain it; but we know it's a life-changing wind.

God gave David this message: *"And it shall be, when thou shalt hear a sound of going in the tops of the mulberry trees, that then thou shalt go out to battle: for God is gone forth before thee to smite the host of the Philistines"* (I Chronicles 14:15). The sound of the wind in the tops of the mulberry trees, the wind of the Spirit, was David's sign. It was God's voice in the wind. Like a wonderful, mighty wind, the Holy Spirit began to blow. David knew it was time to move, and the Lord delivered the Philistines into his hands. Take note of the fact that David waited for the wind of the Spirit, and then he went to claim the promised victory. We must be careful to wait on the Lord.

Paul wasn't in the Upper Room with the rest of the apostles at that time of the outpouring. He was still persecuting believers. But after his conversion he penned these thrilling words: *"That I may know him, and the power of his resurrection, and the fellowship of his sufferings, being made conformable unto his death"* (Philippians 3:10). Those in the Upper Room weren't praying that they might know the power of His resurrection;

they already knew it. It was in the wind. When they came down from the Upper Room, they staggered, fell under the power of the Holy Ghost until the people outside thought they were drunken. The prophecy of Joel came breezing through the wind of the Spirit and fell on Peter, and he began to quote prophecy. *'But this is that which was spoken by the prophet Joel; And it shall come to pass in the last days, saith God, I will pour out of my Spirit upon all flesh"* (Acts 2:16,17).

Sound of the Voice

Ever since Cecil B. DeMille used Charlton Heston's heavily modified voice in his Ten Commandments (1956), the phrase "the voice of God" has become a synonym for "deep male voice." But the voice of God has not always been imagined in this way. At times, the voice of God has been described as that of a parent which could seem benign, benevolent, or terrifying, depending on what kind of relationship you've had with your parents. We are also told that God speaks in a *"still small voice"* (1 Kings 19:12). When the prophet Samuel heard God's voice (1 Samuel 3), it was so ordinary-sounding that Samuel thought it was his teacher Eli. It took God four calls to get the young prophet's full attention. The Bible more often portrays God's voice as sounding ordinary and meek than as booming and thunderous. If God's voice changes to suit the ear of the listener, then the divine word—like the sound of the divine voice itself—may also be open to new, multiple tones and interpretations. If God's image is not exactly in the eye of the beholder—after all, the Bible states that one cannot look at God and live—the sound of God's voice does seem to be in the ear of the listener. According to rabbinic theology, just as Moses experienced God's voice in a certain way, so too, no two individuals experience God in the same fashion.

The Evolving Voice

Beethoven's Fifth is considered one of the world's greatest symphonies. To claim to know exactly what the voice of God sounds like is akin to claiming to know exactly how Beethoven himself meant for this symphony to sound in his day. No one can know with certainty the full meaning and intention of how it should sound as it did in Beethoven's ear. Perhaps he intended it to be played in different ways at different times. In his time, perhaps Beethoven knew that it would be played one way and much later it would evolve into a slightly different sound. As the individual members of an orchestra, the variety of conductors' interpretations of the piece, and the instruments themselves underwent change, its sound would be subtly but noticeably different. It is said that Haydn used the symphony as a vehicle of emotion. But when Beethoven took on the symphony, it only intensified. To this day his symphonies are viewed as brilliant models of how music can express the most powerful of human feelings, in ways that even words can't emulate.

We have evidence, not scientific or historical, but biblical evidence, that just as God was experienced in different ways at different times in history, so too, the sound of God's voice was experienced in different ways at different times in ancient history. Not only is the word of God heard in a plethora of ways, but Jewish tradition suggests the voice of God itself is heard in many different tones. When Moses heard God speak to him for the first time at the burning bush, the ancient rabbis stated that God's voice sounded to Moses like that of his father Amram. According to rabbinic theology, just as Moses experienced God's voice in a certain way, no two individuals experience God in the same fashion. God reveals Himself personally to individuals in a fashion that corresponds to the capacity of each individual listener.

The Decibels of God

Many years ago, by necessity, I was in a position where I had to learn to design, set up, and run an audio and projection system for our church. I had absolutely no experience but had to quickly learn the terminology, technology, and working dynamics of mixing boards, microphones, amplifiers, instruments, EQ frequencies, gain, volume, feedback, and decibels, along with an array of multiple types of connecting wires and cables that make it all run seamlessly. That was another very complex course. But when it comes to speakers and other output devices, the frequency response is measured in decibels of sound pressure. This is roughly interpreted as loudness. Microphones, even though they are detecting sound instead of producing it, are also measured in sensitivity decibels.

Carl Sherman from the Dana Foundation says that hearing is a mechanical sense. It turns physical movement into the electrical signals that make up the language of the brain, translating these vibrations into what we experience as the world of sound. Humans can hear sounds between 0 and 140 decibels. The lower decibel does not mean that there is no sound, merely that we cannot hear it, so zero decibels is the so-called hearing threshold for the human ear.[ii]

A leaf falling to the ground is at ten decibels, but the up-close sound of thunder is at one hundred and thirty decibels. So, the decibels of God fluctuate between the voice of His thunder in the whirlwind (Psalm 77:18), but on Mount Carmel, God speaks at a lower decibel, where Yahweh whispered with a thin silence, which Elijah heard in the cave (1 Kings 19:12). Discerning God's voice in the wind is something like fine-tuning a radio station. The signal is out there, and it is strong and clear, but you must tune precisely into a specific digital frequency to receive a comprehensible signal. All other radio signals must be silenced, or you will be listening to chaos and confusion. So it is in the spirit. While there may be hundreds of choices in radio stations, within yourself there are three basic possible sources of voices: God's voice, the voice of your own soul, or the enemy's suggestions. It is imperative that we distinguish the difference.

No Counterfeits

The truth is, we are born with the capacity for fine-tuning. Jesus said; *"But he who enters by the door is the shepherd of the sheep. To him the doorkeeper opens, and the sheep hear his voice; and he calls his own sheep by name and leads them out. And when he brings out his own sheep, he goes before them; and the sheep follow him, for they know his voice. Yet they will by no means follow a stranger, but will flee from him, for they do not know the voice of strangers"* (John 10:2-5).

Why is it that sheep can so accurately know the voice of the shepherd? Because they have spent large quantities of time with him. And the voice of strangers? They do not follow a stranger's voice because it doesn't resonate with them. If you are one of His sheep, then He is speaking to you and you are hearing His voice! The problem is that we have not learned how to recognize His voice and differentiate it from all the other voices that bombard our hearts and minds.

I understand the way U.S. Treasury workers learn to identify counterfeit bills is not by studying counterfeits, but by handling genuine bills. After a great amount of time in observing and handling the genuine, the counterfeits become obvious. God has been trying to get His people to look, listen and learn the truth for thousands of years. In fact, He gave those exact instructions to an Old Testament king named Ahaz back in the days of the prophet Isaiah. Ahaz was in serious trouble at the time. He had two enemy armies coming against him and he had no idea what to do about it. So, God sent His Word to Ahaz through the prophet Isaiah and gave him a whole new perspective. Instead of agreeing with Ahaz about how powerful his enemies were, God let him know they didn't impress Him much. He referred to them as two "smoking stumps" (Isaiah 7:4, The Amplified Bible). Then He assured Ahaz their plans against him would not stand if he would simply obey the following instructions: Take heed, be quiet, fear not, and believe.

Revelation through Relationship

Before you head down the road looking for a prophet like Isaiah to tell you what God is saying to you, let me save you a trip. You don't need a prophet to tell you what to do. You have a better covenant than Ahaz had. You're not just a servant of God like people were in the Old Covenant. Through the blood of Jesus, you've become a full-fledged son and the Bible says, *"For as many as are led by the Spirit of God, they are the sons of God"* (Romans 8:14). Jesus confirmed that fact in John 10 when He said that His *"sheep hear his voice; and he calls his own sheep by name and leads them out. And when he brings out his own sheep, he goes before them;*

and the sheep follow him, for they know his voice" (John 10:3-4, NKJV). The problem is maturity, not the inability to hear. The problem is that people do not recognize the voice of the Shepherd and easily deceived.

Jesus promised that more revelation would come through the Holy Spirit. There is no end to that revelation, no caveat that says, 'until the Bible is complete.' It is possible that God never intended to limit revelation of who He is to the books of what we call the Old and New Testaments? Should the Bible ever be considered complete anyway? In many ways, I think the Bible has a brand-new set of books being written right now about us partnering with Him in this generation. Jesus always interacted and spoke to His followers. Is it possible that insights today can be progressively added by the Holy Spirit? Jesus said, *"I have many more things to say to you, but you cannot bear them now. But when He, the Spirit of truth, comes, He will guide you into all the truth; for He will not speak on His own initiative, but whatever He hears, He will speak; and He will disclose to you what is to come"* (John 16:12-13)

God never said He was going to communicate with you through your intellect, through your emotions, through your senses, through a sign and wonder, although at times He does. But He did promise to communicate with you through relationship. Therefore, if we desire to hear from God, we do it spirit to spirit, face to face, by looking and listening to what we are sensing in our spirit. You could describe this leading that comes from the Holy Spirit as a sense, a knowing, or by intuition. This happens when God shows you something inside your heart or you hear something from God in your spirit. Jesus heard from the Father in this manner. In Mark 2:8 it says, *"Jesus perceived in his spirit."* In John 6:61 it says, *"Jesus knew in himself."* Jesus isn't hearing something with his physical ear, but rather He is getting direction through His spirit. The reality is we are supposed to be hearing from God in this same way every day of our lives through relationship.

Tuning in to God's Frequency

Have you ever lost a child in a crowd? What a scary feeling it is! You immediately begin calling their name until you find them, only to find out they were never too far away, just hidden by people far taller than themselves. They couldn't see us, but they could hear our voices calling. Your voice heard by the child brought hope, security, direction, and peace. So it is with God. We develop an "ear" for those we love the most through relationship. A mother will recognize the voice of her child. Likewise, a child will know what a mother is saying, although she does not speak. With a single look from her eye, she can speak volumes.

Likewise, God can speak to us on many different heavenly frequencies. It's through deep relationship we align ourselves in a position of being tuned to hear His voice on different levels. Understanding how He speaks is the first step to discerning His voice. Christianity is unique among all other religions because it offers a personal relationship with the Creator, beginning here and now in this world, then lasting throughout eternity. As Jesus declared, *This is eternal life – that they may know God"* (Jn. 17:2). Often, we think of His voice as coming from the outside, maybe an audible voice, or through someone else or from somewhere else. No matter how it comes, the voice of the Lord will approach as a friend. It often appears from within because He lives within, spirit to spirit. It comes as an internal desire that is activated as He speaks. When we recognize the power of God's love, we are encouraged to open ourselves up to Him to grow into a deeper relationship with Him. I want everything that God will give the human spirit in this age.

The Bible describes humans as tripartite beings, having three parts; spirit, soul, and body. John Paul Jackson further delineates this by saying that each of these three parts has three parts. Spirit is made up of wisdom, communion, and conscience. Soul (or mind) is made up of intellect, emotion, and will. The body is made up of flesh, blood, and bone. To grasp an understanding of each, we can say that the body gives us world consciousness through the five senses of touch, smell, sight, taste and hearing. We are conscious of the world around us through the five senses. The soul or mind gives us self-consciousness.

We know ourselves better than anyone else and it's through our memories and past events that we have our mind, or soul shaped.

The human spirit then, gives us a God consciousness. The only way to truly know God is by the spirit, God's spirit in communion with our spirit. *"God is Spirit and they that worship Him must worship Him in spirit and in truth"* (John 4:24). In other words, you cannot worship God by the soul or the body without the spirit. I believe that when our spirit is leading our worship of God, the soul and the body will naturally follow. That is why we are commanded in Deuteronomy 6:5 to *"love or worship God with all our heart, soul, and strength."* Heart for spirit, soul for mind, and strength for body. Even Jesus needed the Holy Spirit.

The Puritan John Owen had an insightful way of explaining the relation of Christ's two natures. To my knowledge, this had not been as clearly articulated by anyone before him. One of his chief concerns was to protect the integrity of Christ's two natures (divine and human). In so doing, he made a rather bold contention that the only singular immediate act of the Son of God (the divine second person) on the human nature of Christ was the decision to take it into subsistence with himself in the incarnation. Every other act upon Christ's human nature was from the Holy Spirit.[iii]

Mystical Connection

The discipline of worshipping God in the spirit has sometimes been called a mystic connection to God or simply mysticism. In conservative Christian circles, one may hear that we should avoid mysticism, mainly because it suggests, for many, eastern spiritism, which is vastly different. Eastern mysticism involves the worship or connection to something other than the One true God. In all times and places there have been those who seek to escape the bonds of flesh and ascend to be united with God. In Christian teaching, God descended into flesh to make that union possible. This gives a unique character to Christian mysticism, the only religion whose founder is believed to be God Himself come to earth and with whom followers may still enter into communion. Early Christians believed and understood mysticism to be the only way to connect to God. In fact, a lot of the deep spiritual writings of these early Christians are called the writings of the mystics. Saint John of the Cross, Francis of Assisi, Teresa of Avila, and Brother Lawrence, just to name a few. We have books from many of these ancient writings in our personal library.

The earliest documents of the Christian church were written by a mystic: they are the letters of the Apostle Paul. As a writer, Paul based his apostolic authority not on having encountered Jesus in the flesh, but rather on the road to Damascus. And he seemed to wish that every Christian could have the same interior sense of the love of God "that surpasses knowledge" (Eph 3. 19). Technically speaking, Paul's experience on the road to Damascus was more a theophany, a physical manifestation, than a vision, since all three accounts in the chapter of Acts note that others in Paul's traveling party saw a great light or heard a sound, though only he heard the words Jesus spoke.

Apart from his experience on the road to Damascus, Paul also speaks of a mystical ascent into "the third heaven," whether in the body or out of it he did not know, where he heard inexpressible things which he is not permitted to tell. (II Corinthians 12:1-10) Paul seems to have broached this topic reluctantly. He speaks of his experience in the third person and moves quickly from his "surpassingly great revelation" (12:7) to his own weakness. Where some readers might find Paul's epistles "inspirational" in the generic sense of providing moral uplift, mystical interpreters take his words at face value. For example, when Paul writes, *"God's love has been poured into our hearts through the Holy Spirit which has been given to us"* (Rom 5.5, RSV), the words, perhaps dulled by over-familiarity, sound like the kind of rhetorical flourish one hears in church services. But for Christian mystics through the ages, this is a promise that may be taken quite literally.

In any case, as we open to Him, we experience and share in God's love, the love that poured from the cross. Something special happens in our hearts, our souls, our entire beings when we open up to that love. Something that is difficult to explain…without the idea of the resonant frequency.

The Frequency of Love

We are most certainly created with a resonant frequency, and that frequency is the love of God, which is God Himself - since God is love. When our lives are disrupted and shaken by the frequency of God's love, our entire being resonates. It resonates far more than anything else trying to shake us. That resonance is worship. So often we make worship out to be something it's not. It's not about the music, the person singing on stage, the positions of raised hands, the fancy light show or lack thereof, or the awkwardness of not caring what anyone thinks. Worship is about the position of the heart. If that position is open to God, we begin resonating with His love. We may feel at times that a segment of worship was shallow and meaningless for us. Maybe we're simply not allowing ourselves to resonate with God's love because of the burden of external pressures of everyday life we were never meant to carry.

For several years now, the Father has been releasing a sound from heaven designed to connect to the deep desire within us all for both relationship and responsibility. It is represented within much of the music being performed today by Christian musicians. But it is not itself necessarily an audible sound to the human or natural ear by a cry from within the spirit. Some have heard it in the spirit and responded already, but that sound frequency continues to intensify, encouraging all His children to be spiritually open and sensitive and to resonate with it. Let it penetrate as deep calls to deep to awaken your sonship. As you become aware of it, learn to rest and relax in it, to be immersed in His presence, and to resonate with His intention for your life as that is conveyed to you in the sound.

For the most part, the frequency is one of a calling for us as His children to come and take our places in heaven; to find and fulfill our heavenly roles so that we can bring heaven to earth through our lives. The Father has given His children a destiny that involves our inheritance and birthright so that we can all be mature sons of God, revealed out of heaven into the earth. He is always giving us opportunity to come to Him to obtain a deeper revelation of our identity, position and authority.

The point of God speaking in the still small voice was to show Elijah that the work of God need not always be accompanied by dramatic revelation or manifestations. Divine silence does not necessarily mean divine inactivity. Zechariah 4:6 tells us that God's work is *"not by might nor by power, but by My Spirit,"* meaning that overt displays of power are not necessary for God to work.

Because He is God, He is not confined to a single manner of communicating with His people. Elsewhere in Scripture, He is said to communicate through a whirlwind (Job 38:1), to announce His presence by an earthquake (Exodus 19:18), and to speak in a voice that sounds like thunder (1 Samuel 2:10; Job 37:2; Psalm 104:7; John 12:29). In Psalm 77:18 His voice is compared to both thunder and a whirlwind. And in Revelation 4:5, we're told that lightning and thunder proceed from the throne in heaven.

God is not limited to natural phenomena when He speaks. All through Scripture, He speaks through His prophets over and over. The common thread in all the prophets is the phrase, "Thus says the Lord." He speaks through the writers of Scripture. Most graciously, however, He speaks through His Son, the Lord Jesus. The writer to the Hebrews opens his letter with this truth: *"Long ago, at many times and in many ways, God spoke to our fathers by the prophets, but in these last days he has spoken to us by his Son, whom he appointed the heir of all things, through whom also he created the world"* (Hebrews 1:1–2).

The difference between God speaking through the thunder and the whirlwind, then through the still, small voice, can be also considered as showing the difference between the two dispensations of law and grace. The law is a voice of terrible words and was given amidst a tempest of wind, thunder, and lightning, attended by an earthquake (Hebrews 12:18–24). But the gospel is a gentle voice of love, grace, and mercy, of peace, pardon, righteousness, and the free gift of salvation through Christ. The law breaks the rocky hearts of men in pieces, shakes their consciences, and fills their minds with a sense of God's fiery wrath and the punishment they deserve, and then the gospel speaks gently to them of the peace and pardon available in Christ.

Creation is Groaning

Investiture, succession, enthronement, coronation are words that describe the process of a king coming into the fullness of his power and authority. We are invested with authority as sons of God but for there to be succession, the old king must either die or abdicate. The old king in this context is our soul, in the sense that it has been controlling our lives which was never its intended purpose. Then we can take up our throne in heaven (enthronement) and be recognized by creation as the sons we truly are (coronation).

The decibels of the groan of Creation in its bondage to corruption and decay (Rom 8:22) are increasing. That groan demands an answer and we, the sons of God, are the only ones who can supply it. We are called to administrate and oversee the fruitfulness and increase which come from the face-to-face restored innocence of relationship, not the decay and death which are the consequences of independence.

Nothing changes by itself without the necessary adjustments in the spirit. With the correct identity, alignment and purpose, we effectively bring about the change as God's representatives on the earth. As mature sons, when we hear or see in the realm of the spirit, it may seem as though we are receiving information and revelation, not knowing how to apply it. However, I believe the Word of the Lord hovers in the atmosphere until we discover and apply it to what already exists. I am reminded of a scripture, Isaiah 55:11, *"...so is my word that goes out from my mouth: It will not return to me empty but will accomplish what I desire and achieve the purpose for which I sent it."*
A mature son hears the voice, aligns his heart with the word, and declares it over the earth, fulfilling God's original intent. When the word is released, it has a supernatural power to change conditions, circumstances, and atmospheres that ultimately can shift a nation.

Today, the Holy Spirit is being released in a way that will bring purity to the body of Christ and release the authority, power, and glory of the Lord in such an unprecedented way that even the creation itself will begin to respond.

CHAPTER THREE

Our Reformed DNA

How many have prayed, listened, and fasted, wanting to hear God speak, yet not hearing anything? And how many were driving down the road not thinking about anything when suddenly God speaks? What is the difference? Why does God speak when we are seemingly not paying attention or fervently praying with great intent? Why is it that we will hear His voice when we are not focused in that direction? I believe the difference is that we often try to hear God speak with our natural minds. But God speaks spirit to spirit. In essence, *"the natural person does not accept the things of the Spirit of God, for they are folly to him, and he is not able to understand them because they are spiritually discerned"* (I Cor. 2:14, ESV).

While many devout Christians see a woman's function as a subordinate to a man, the word *ezer* in the original Hebrew overturns that idea. The woman was not created to serve the man, but to serve with the man. Without the woman, the man was only half the story. She was not an afterthought or an optional adjunct to an independent, self-sufficient man. God said in Genesis 2:18 that without her, the man's condition was "not good."

The noun form, נגד (neged), is often used for one thing that is face-to-face with something else. We find an example in Genesis 21:16 where Hagar went and sat down "opposite" her son. Even though she and her son are far away, they are sitting "face to face." That is the context. Putting all of this together, the phrase עזר כנגדו (Ezer kenegedo) means "a helper like his opposite." In my opinion, this means that Eve was to be Adam's "other half," like him, but with the opposite attributes. In other words, a mirror image.

You might wonder what this has to do with hearing God's voice? Let's go back to Genesis 3 and look at the voice in the garden. In

Genesis 3:8, when Adam heard the voice of God walking in the garden, it says he heard something internally. Listen, this is speaking of Adam and Eve walking in the garden, when they heard the voice of the Lord walking in the garden. How many have ever heard a voice walking? That's a bit unusual, right? In the cool of the day, Adam and his wife hid themselves from the presence of the Lord amongst the trees of the garden. And the Lord calls out in verse 9, the Lord called unto Adam, and said to him, *"Where art thou?"* In other words, where did you go Adam? Adam replied in verse 10 *"I heard your voice in the garden and I was afraid because I was naked, and I hid myself."*

I want you to hear those words, "when they heard the voice of the Lord walking in the garden in the cool of the day." They heard the voice and suddenly became fearful and hid themselves from the presence. They hid themselves amongst the trees of the garden and then God asks Adam, "Where are you Adam?" Adam said he heard the voice and was afraid and hid himself because he knew he was naked. Who told him that before? Who told him he didn't have a conscience? He was created a pure spirit. He was perfect in every way, because God created him in His image. How was it that they could hear the sound of the voice of the Lord walking? How can a voice walk?

Notice, God called him out by name. God calls out, "Adam! Where are you?" He's speaking to his identity. Whenever God calls you out by name, He's speaking to your identity. It's not like God did not know where Adam was. He was not asking Adam about his location. He was asking Adam, What condition do you find yourself in? How about our relationship, Adam? Where is your mind? What happened to our relationship? Why are you where you are? At what point do you think you can hide in the trees like a monkey? That's kind of what he implied when He asked, why are you hiding amongst the trees? We never did this before Adam.

Again, God was not asking Adam about his location. He wanted Adam to identify where his mind was. What happened to you Adam, that you had a state of mind change? His identity had been lost! Adam replies, "I heard your voice and I was afraid, so I hid myself." What did Adam hear? He heard the voice of the Lord walking. He didn't hear the voice of God talking. His voice stirs and walks in the cool of the day. This voice walks and moves. The word voice here means in this instance; wind, exhale, as to breathe. The Hebrew word Panim for presence, as in "I hid myself from your presence because I was afraid" actually means face or face-in-face. "I hid myself from Your face, I could no longer see your face in my face" If we were to put it in modern English, it would read more like this, I heard your sound walking in the wind of the day, so I hid myself from Your face, from Your image, from Your presence, because I was afraid. This is a voice that moves on the wind. Adam chose to hide himself from the image of God because of fear and yet he had an ability of facing God. He was created with an ability to stand face to face with God. That's what he lost.

In Whose Image Are You?

Presently, some people's spirituality is hidden amongst the trees, meaning they have an inferior image, thinking they're not qualified to speak for God. Certainly, they cannot speak for Him if they are full of fear. So, I ask the question, if you are not created in His image and likeness, in whose image, are you? Where is your mind? Are you so trapped by your failures that you cannot accept where you are? Are you so overcome with your defeats that you have become a prisoner within your own identity? Or, are you free as a son who knows his image?

Consider this illustration: If I were to take an eraser (which must be a supernatural eraser) and I began by erasing your face and then moved on to your hair and toes, and then continued by erasing your false eyelashes and your plastic nails. After erasing your gender, I move on to erase all your past failures and all your goodness. I would erase all your thoughts and return you to your mother's womb. And then I'd erase that too. Now, where are you? You are now at the place where you are in the heart of the heavenly Father. What do you have left? What would we find? Right at that point, God would be the only thing left. You are in His heart. That's who you are! That's from where you came! You are in His image. People begin hiding when they lose their identity in Christ. It's where they withdraw and hide amongst the trees. In biblical imagery, trees often speak of humanity. Remember the man who got his eyesight healed in Mark 10:46-52? He said, *"I see men as trees walking."*

Finding Your Identity

People withdraw when they lose their identity. They start drawing away from transparency, fearing exposure and rushing to hide in the crowd. They seem to evaporate in religion because they have become more convinced of their failures than the greatness of what God has done for them. Adam and Eve were found hiding amongst the trees. If your church talks more about sin than what Jesus did for you, get out of that place. God already appointed you as an overcomer! People who lose their identity pull away from God and life. They become entangled in the Tree of the Knowledge of Good and Evil. Remember, Adam could eat of the Tree of Life, but he chose to eat of the Tree of the Knowledge of Good and Evil. Our identities must be rooted in God's ability and identity, not our own. The deepest longing of the human heart is to know and enjoy the glory of God. We were made for this. *"Bring my sons from afar and my daughters from the end of the earth . . . whom I created for my glory,"* says the Lord (Isaiah 43:6–7). To see it, to savor it, and to show it—that is why we exist.

When you are having a good day, you feel like a son, right? But on a bad day, you don't lose your identity as a son. A perfect example is the story of the prodigal son. His father was actively engaged in looking for his return. There was a grand celebration upon his homecoming. Family identity is not canceled based on your feelings but determined by DNA. God did not put parameters on your identity. He said, you are my son! Your DNA is at the core of your being, and it doesn't matter what you think you are because your DNA is uniquely locked in you. Your DNA somewhat determines your outcome. If you are born again, God has placed His DNA in you; therefore, you are His son if He is your father. Women are included as sons because the spirit has no gender. His DNA within doesn't disappear based on your feelings or gender, no matter your culture.

The extremists in our American culture right now are struggling to push gender confusion on society. It's obvious to determine who you are in gender, male or female. Just because you have mixed emotions or confusion doesn't change your gender. Radical extremists propagate gender confusion because they want to break down and destroy the family unit and the structures God placed and set in order. Do you know what God does? He laughs at His enemies' attempts. God is not intimidated by the resistors because He is determined to have His sons come to maturity. He will have a remnant and some overcomers that work with Him, and they will change the world together.

Moving into Maturity

The time has come for the Body of Christ to move beyond momentary encounters and into a place of habitation, a place of dwelling in order that the full measure of Holy Spirit that rested and remained on Jesus begins to manifest in our lives every day. As mature sons, our call is to enjoy participation with God as He brings heaven to earth through us. We birth substance from the invisible realm into the visible world around us. Much like Mary, the church is to be a womb to conceive the substance of God's purpose and then give birth to a tangible expression of Christ in the earth.

Our goal is not to merely learn about the nature of the Spirit but to be fully possessed by Him with the authority and power of heaven backing us. The job description of a true believer is to not simply be a hearer of the Word but a doer of the Word. That means our lives are to manifest physical signposts of unseen heavenly realities. God is raising up a generation to meet this task. A church that will both understand and appropriate the mysteries of heaven. This is a body of people who will comprehend the hidden things of His Kingdom, and they will also demonstrate His power for the world to take notice.

There is a company of believers on the rise who will literally shine forth the fullness of God. The Kingdom of God is not about better church meetings. Holy Spirit wants to work individually through you to release the substance of the Kingdom throughout society. Whatever your sphere of influence is, He wants to move on that. If you are an artist, He wants to paint on the canvas of others' lives with the medium of His love through you. He is not looking for a more productive church, He is looking for an intimacy-driven church.

God Himself chooses weak, foolish, and insignificant things to shame the wise, mighty, and strong things of this world so that no flesh will glory in His presence (1 Corinthians 1:27–29). To empower us, He chooses things for us like speaking to an invisible Person, fasting, and giving away money as the methods of releasing His power. This does not make any sense to our natural minds, but it is the operating principle of His kingdom. God designed His government to be released through a partnership. He chooses the simplicity of intercession because He desires relationship. God doesn't do things alone. He awakens human beings, calls them into friendship, and then through their prayers and lives - they manifest the things hidden in His heart.

I believe we are living in the days now where God is bringing the Body of Christ back to this original paradigm of governance. He is calling believers back to the realities of the Garden in Eden, to walk in that sacred place of connection with Him we are filled with the knowledge of His will and empowered to speak and release His desires. The Kingdom of God is not about what you do. The Kingdom is mostly about who you are. The Kingdom is about what you represent and the authority you carry while walking on the face of the earth.

The Plurality of God

The plurality of God is humanity. That is a big statement. God duplicated Himself in humanity. Genesis 1:27 says, *"So God created mankind in his image and in the image of God he created them male and female."* He created them, and He called them Adam. At the beginning of the creation process, Adam possessed the qualities of both male and female. Meaning he was created whole with spirit and soul. Later, when Adam became self-conscious at the fall, the soul and spirit were divided and ripped apart. Partaking of the Knowledge of the Tree of Good and Evil meant Adam would need his soul restored through a perfected God-man named Christ Jesus, the last Adam. The Adamic race ended, and a new creation of god-man was born. Christ came in you and you became a new creation. The old man is dead and there's a new man upon the scene. The problem is not the old Adam, the problem is with the immature new man that doesn't know the truth because so many teachers focus on what's wrong with you. It's time to discover what's right with you! We've had so many religious leaders tell us You can't do this, you can't do that. Yes, you can!

All the promises of God are yay and amen. But you've got to pursue Him with all your heart. You've got to go after Him with all your passion. I want to possess the same love that branded me. I want to apprehend and pursue Him with the same love that apprehended and pursued me. I want to know Him in the fullness of His grace. I want to know Him and the fullness of His spirit. I need to know Him in the fullness of His mind. I've got to have the power of transformation. I'm not interested in religion and I'm not interested in the ambition of ministry. I'm not interested in doing something for God. I just want God! I want the fullness of His spirit resting on me!

A representation of the soul and spirit was on display when Eve was taken from the side of Adam. In biblical symbolism, the spirit is referred to as masculine in gender. The soul then is feminine in gender. But the reconstruction of God's plan in Eden's Garden caused by disobedience reversed God's original intentions, leading to a dying spirit and a fracture in the soul. Consequentially, God had to put them back together through the perfect work of Christ. That's a different message, and I can't go into it here but it's worth looking into.

The Focus is Changing

The Holy Spirit is going to shift the focus of the end-time Church. I'm prophesying to you now, but with the scriptures behind me, it's pretty easy to get this prophecy right. The Holy Spirit is going to shift the primary focus of the end-time Church away from being primarily concerned with getting more influence and more things. He's going to make that second. He's going to shift the focus of the heart to experiencing God's heart and then to giving our heart back to Him in fullness. God is calling His children, His sons, to come out of the wilderness. He is calling His sons to cross over into their supernatural inheritance beyond the veil. He is calling His sons into deeper levels of intimacy, calling us to know Him. As you begin to respond, you may find that He uncovers areas of brokenness and fragmentation within your soul which require healing and restoration. Don't resist that; go with it. I recommend you journal everything the Father speaks to you as He reveals His truth and heals your wounds. "I want my Sons to wake up!" This is the cry from the Father's heart - to unveil, reveal and release His children into their full, glorious identity and inheritance as mature sons of God: the Elohim, god-like ones.

It is also the groan of all creation which is longing to be set free when we are matured and revealed. Through the intimacy of a deeper relationship with the Father, let's embrace our destinies as sons: let's answer the groan of creation by revealing the true nature of God and the true essence of love expressed in our glorious freedom.

'Sons' is not gender-specific. We are all children of God who have an inheritance and are training in the family business. As sons, we are included in the circle of relationship that is Father, Son and Spirit, reconnected to the true reality of God's original intention for our identity and destiny. However, we cannot be recognized as sons until we recognize that we have a Father.

The Scribe who was writing about Samuel's life wrote, "the Lord did not let any of his words fall to the Ground." I love that! You know what that means? It means partnership with God. The situation here is as though God was saying, "I've got your back! You've proven yourself faithful enough to me even if you don't get it quite perfect, I won't let your words fall to the ground." God has such confidence in a son that he wants to share in his reputation and works such that he's allowing us the authority to say things and even get it wrong and he'll still back us up. That is the inheritance of sons.

When we engage with the Father in this earthly realm under an open heaven, we can also be affirmed as sons. You can hear the Father speak to you as He spoke to Jesus at His baptism: *"You are my son; in you I am well pleased. My soul delights in you."* In today's vernacular, it would read as this; "Receive My acceptance, affirmation, approval, recognition; receive My recommendation, commendation, blessing, endorsement, and validation." When you hear Him speak words like that to you, you don't fight against them or argue with Him. What He speaks over you is the truth, receive it.

Jesus went on to have further experiences of engaging with His Father in this realm. It got to the point where He began to shine. He demonstrated what sonship looks like by being transfigured, radiating the light of God. As sons, we will do the same and it is already happening for some. Don't limit the possibilities. As you engage with the Father, He is transforming you. Transform and transfigure are translations of the same Greek word. You are being changed from one degree of glory to another: from human beings to living beings, to spirit beings, to godlike beings. Let me be clear, we are not replacing God – we are walking in His image, replicating heaven on earth. *"And the child grew and was strengthened in spirit, being filled with wisdom, and the grace of God was upon him… And Jesus kept increasing in wisdom and stature, and in favor with God and men."* (Lk 2:40, 52). The more we engage with the Father, the more we will grow and mature in wisdom and grace.

God's Concept of Rulership

God's concept of rulership could be shocking if you are living in the United States. There is a concept that is not supported by the Constitution, but it is accepted in the mindset of the American psyche, that is the separation of church and state. God has no concept about the separation of church and state because when He created Adam, he was both church and state in one body. The church is simply the spiritual representative and government is the royal kingly administrative representative. God's original purpose was for each human to be a king and a priest. This is very important because politicians have keep pushing them apart to the point where some have accepted that it's not good for a Christian to be involved in civil government. We have people standing in the pulpits of Christian churches preaching against believers getting involved in politics because the concept has been sold by the enemy into our minds that you cannot be both.

The word *king* means ruler. A ruler is the executive branch of a government. The king deals with rights. So, a king is the executive branch of government that deals with executing legislation. Keep in mind that the government structure of Europe grew out of the Roman structure under which Christ was born. The word king is the same word as ruler in the Hebrew and Greek languages. This is important because the Bible says, *"God created man and said to him, have dominion over the earth."*

Adam was created to be a ruler or a dominator of the earth. He was created to be the executive of the earth – to execute God's government purposes in the earth. Adam therefore was the king of the earth and his children are all kings of the earth. God intended for kings to deal with rights, and a right is a judgment based on law. Man was given the assignment by God to rule earth and to execute God's righteous judgments on earth. That means to give the earth what is rightfully its own.

A priest is an interesting part of the government because the priest is the spiritual branch of God's government. The word priest also means a representative of God. Both faculties are representatives, but the priest is the spiritual branch and the priest deals with righteousness. A king deals with rights and a priest deals with righteousness and relationship. The king deals with power executing judgment, and the priest branch deals with staying in relationship with the government. We are kings and priests according to God's original intent.

Reformed DNA

When you received the Gospel of the Kingdom, your Adamic DNA was replaced by the heavenly Father's eternal DNA. Not long ago, scientists discovered a third strand in the human DNA. Often, we see DNA as looking like a twisted ladder-like construct, with little steps in between. For years, we only saw two sides of the ladder. Now it's been discovered that there's an invisible third strand they can't see, yet they know it's there. This can only have one explanation: The God particle, because it's light. It's light they can't see that's holding everything together.

As the ecclesia, we are God's kingdom ambassadors on earth. Without us, creation cannot hear. Creation can't hear because there's no mouth to speak what God already said. There's a frequency in every solid object that responds to the voice of God. We cannot determine this from science, but from a spirit of revelation. All matter consists of atoms made of protons, neutrons, and electrons. Atoms stick together to form molecules, the building blocks for matter densities. Every piece of matter has a resonance frequency or series of frequencies because of the vibration of the atoms. Atoms are formed by electromagnetic waves that have a specific frequency. When these atoms form a larger piece of matter, the frequency of the electromagnetic waves is the frequency of that matter. There are subatomic particles that form to create atoms. They are in everything and vibrate at different speeds depending on the density of the matter. A discovery in the actions of force particles has recently transformed the study of subatomic particles, in that they are due to the exchange of "force" particles.

CHAPTER FOUR

Force Particles

Early in the 20th century the unquestioned assumption that the physical universe is actually physical led to a scientific search for the elementary "point particle" upon which all life is built, which would prove that reality was not an illusion. But as soon as scientists began smashing electrons and other particles in enormous accelerators, they quickly realized the foundations of the physical world weren't physical at all—that everything is energy. [iv]

God's word then, is like a force particle in the spiritual realm that changes and influences the natural. His creative Word has the power and energy to smash through all resistance to yield up what it was sent to accomplish. His energy behind His Word displaces all other energy forms both in the spirit realm and the natural. God is spirit, and He needs a mouth that agrees with His purpose to declare and release a word to change creation. God says, "Here's how I move. I move upon the winds that carry My exhale. My creative power is in that wind. It's also in the breath of one who believes Me."

When a mature son speaks on behalf of God, His father, creation cannot distinguish the difference in the voice, whether God the Father or the son speak, because it's the same. Creation doesn't know if it's God's voice or a man's voice as long as the breath or wind carries the sound frequency of God's voice.

Think of it this way. When Noah, under the command of God, gathered two of every life form species on the earth, he did it by speaking a word, and they came to him. He didn't have to go hunting and round up all the donkeys, camels, and giraffes. He spoke out a word that had the sound of God on the earth, and creation responded to it. God put the authority of His words in Noah's mouth, making a powerful sound. Noah agreed with the word of God, and he spoke to creation, and they came to him. That's what we need to be doing right now. Things come to us because we carry the sound of God's voice, His frequency, and speak into creation. The more we engage with the Father, the more we are transfigured and transformed, growing and maturing in wisdom and grace. The first dimension in which we engage is in the Earth, the physical realm, but in the spiritual atmosphere of an open heaven.

Convergence of Time and Eternity

The cloud of His Presence, the cloud of the Father's glory, comes around us and God speaks to us from where He is, out of eternity. Truth will be revealed to us from His perspective, not necessarily ours. That is why I suggest we do not try to figure it all out or try to understand it, just to receive. Your spirit will receive and digest it, and the Holy Spirit will bring it to your mind when you need it. All creation recognizes the frequency in the voice of the Father. The son carries the same frequency because the wind or the breath of God rides upon it. So, whether it comes from the father or the son doesn't matter because the two are one. All creation will respond to it. That is our promise. That is the awesomeness of the God we partner with. That is who has placed his DNA in you. Jesus invites us to open the door in our spirit to allow the presence of God to fill us. When our spirit is full, that presence overflows and fills the garden of our heart, fills our soul with His presence. This is essential to the promise that follows, that we will be seated with Him on His throne, exercising authority and participating in the government of the Kingdom. So, I ask the question: Are we content to remain earthbound, restricted, living in a carefully constructed illusion that reduces us to mere mortals? Or are we going to step into what has been given to us and begin the process of the restoration of all things as He promised?

New Strategies

Have you ever stopped to question how much of what we believe is because we have always believed it, based on what someone else has taught us, or from a religious construct, doctrine or theology? How much is derived from or influenced by our culture and society? And finally, how much is from revelation, coming out of our direct personal experience of relationship with God Himself? In short, how much are we 'leaning to our own understanding'?

The Joshua generation was a forerunner of the new in Israel's history just as we are the Joshua generation for the present. We are finding a new level of experiential relationship with God, a new level of communication with Him, new ability to hear and see what He reveals. We are finding out what it means to have the mind of Christ! God is calling us to let go of the old and embrace the new: new mindsets and new paradigms, new worldviews.

We must not be surprised if we encounter great resistance to change, and not only from the quarters we might expect. Certainly, some people in the old established churches will oppose what God is doing, but the greater resistance will likely come from more recent moves of God which have settled into a maintenance mode. God has begun challenging the very pillars of understanding in our minds. We are in a time now of transition, of uncertainty and change.

Divergence, Convergence, and Emergence

Divergence is akin to the inhale of a breath, the convergence phase is affiliated with holding your breath, and emergence is associated with the exhalation of a breath. Learning to hear from God involves taking a breath and spending quality contemplating time with God. The outcome is a radical supernatural moment.[v] The emergence process encompasses seeing from a different perception. When you were born again, you were joined to God's Spirit with a spiritual ability to hear God, which was put into your DNA: *"That which is born of the flesh is flesh, and that which is born of the Spirit is spirit."* (John 3:6). The human spirit is now joined face-to-face with the Spirit of God as an alongside one. And when Jesus was ready to ascend to the Father, He says, *"I will pray the Father, and He will give you another Helper, that He may abide with you forever"* (John 14:16).

You never know when the Spirit will speak, but you can create an environment where the Spirit does speak. Greek thought views the world through the mind (abstract thought), while ancient Hebrew thought views the world through the senses (concrete thought). The Hebrew concrete thought is the expression of concepts and ideas in ways that can be seen, touched, smelled, tasted, or heard. Through similes and metaphors, the Hebrew writers paint pictures to clarify God's truth. Psalm 1:3 illustrates the concrete with a simile when it says, *"the godly are like a tree planted by streams of water."* Psalm 29 is a dominant example of how the Hebrew, David, used poetic, metaphorical language to express the power and energy of God's voice. *"At the voice of Your thunder, they hastened away."*

In a Psalm where the voice of the Lord is emphasized seven times, the only word spoken is reserved for those in the temple, which is filled with His glory. When God speaks, glory is revealed. The paralyzing description of God's thundering voice now begins with one of the first sudden transitions, which David loves: The voice of the Lord is upon the waters— the heavenly exhibition of Jehovah's power, which is the support of the opening call to worship. His voice is heard in the pealing of the thunder above the storm clouds, like it was on the mountain of God.

Nothing changes by itself without the necessary adjustments in the spirit. With the correct identity, alignment and purpose, we effectively bring about the change as God's representatives on the earth. As mature sons, when we hear or see in the realm of the spirit, it may seem as though we are receiving information and revelation, not always knowing how to apply it. However, I believe the Word of the Lord hovers in the atmosphere until we discover and apply it to what already exists. I am reminded of a scripture, Isaiah 55:11, *"...so is my word that goes out from my mouth: It will not return to me empty but will accomplish what I desire and achieve the purpose for which I sent it."*

A mature son hears the voice, aligns his heart with the word, and declares it over the earth, fulfilling God's original intent. When the word is released, it has a supernatural power to change conditions, circumstances, and atmospheres that ultimately shift a nations' direction. Today the Holy Spirit is being released in a way that will bring purity to the body of Christ and release the authority, power, and glory of the Lord in such an unprecedented way that even the creation itself will begin to respond.

Central to our identity in Christ is that we are children of God. First, we are born again unto salvation through which we enter eternal life. And second, we grow by the spirit of adoption through which we become mature sons and daughters of God. The Greek word in John 1:12 and 1 John 3:1 is "teknon," which refers to a child or newly born believer. In contrast, the Greek "huios" used in the passages in Romans 8:14-19 and Galatians 4:7 denotes a mature, adult son heir to his father's name and authority, possessions, and responsibilities. As children of God, we possess the right of inheritance, but as mature sons and daughters, we hold the key to access treasures. Mature sons go about their Father's business by accomplishing God's purposes. Jesus did not come just that we might have life, but that we might have life more abundantly (John 10:10). He did not come just that we might be born unto salvation, but that we might also grow into mature spiritual sons and daughters fully equipped to realize His purposes in the earth.

God's breath is full of power, creative energy, and life. That is the voice in the wind. *"By the word of the LORD the heavens were made, their starry host by the breath of his mouth."* (Psalm 33:6) When God created the universe, He first framed up the universe by exhaling His desire. God builds from a place of rest with His word. When God speaks, His word carries out His every bidding. His word is controlling this universe and holding the elements together.

God is a Spirit and He wanted us to see Him, know Him, to understand how we are to operate on the earth, so He sent a representative of Himself, Jesus Christ, the Son of God! Jesus is the representative of the substance of God. When you look at Jesus and His life, you see a picture of what the Father is like. God wanted all of

Himself to be in His Son. Throughout the life and ministry of Jesus, He only spoke the creative, life-giving words of His Father.

Common people witnessed and recognized the power and authority of Jesus' word in action. *"For the creation eagerly waits for the revelation of the sons of God"* (Rom. 8:19, NET). Words were the instruments by which God created all things. Nine times the words, "And God said" appears in Genesis chapter one. Each time God spoke, something was created, formed, or made. Worlds came into being, planets and stars were born, and the synchronicity and timing of a universe was beautifully coordinated, and now exist by the command of God.

Creation was established by God's words and responded to the words spoken by Jesus. With faith-filled words, Jesus calmed the raging sea, raised the widow's son, and called Lazarus from the tomb. Jesus spoke creative words to the man with the withered hand. Jesus spoke words of healing to the woman with the spirit of infirmity. To the paralytic, Jesus' words were directional, *"Take up thy bed."* In Matthew 8:5-13, the centurion, knowing the authority and power of Jesus' words, proclaimed, *"Only speak the word and my servant shall be healed."* The power of God's word is on your lips and in your mouth. In Isaiah's vision, the seraphim took a live coal from the altar and placed it on Isaiah's mouth. This symbolized Isaiah's cleansing, sins being forgiven. (Isaiah 6:6–7).

God made us in His image so that we could act like Him. To be Christ-like is to walk maturely as a son. At creation, God gave man dominion and authority over the works of His hands. This dominion was to be exercised through a son's words. Authority in any area is exercised through words. God created and upheld all things by His word. Creation responded to those words spoken by Jesus. Now, as sons, dominion has been given to us and creation will likewise respond to the words spoken by us when in alignment with the Father's heart.

One key is Jesus only spoke what He heard from the Father. God has given us the authority and ability to change things so that we can control and remove anything that stands in the way of the will of God being done. Isaiah wrote, God performs the words of His servants.

"Thus saith the Lord, thy Redeemer…I am the Lord…Who confirms the word of His servant" (Isaiah 44:24-26). Confirm is defined as to make good, perform, establish, make to stand, to make effective, to bind by some formal or legal act, to substantiate, to affirm as having substance, to demonstrate, to verify. Perform is defined as making prosperous, making good, carrying out, or executing. Execute is defined as carrying into effect, fulfilling a command, promise, undertaking, carrying out an order, or carrying through a plan or program. Notice, God did not say, "I confirm the word of My apostle, evangelist, prophet, pastor, or teacher." He said, "I perform the word of My servant."

Elijah stopped the rain for three and a half years with words. When your words agree with God's word, they do not return to you void, but they accomplish that for which you and God sent them. Jesus said, "We are one." Therefore, when your words agree with God, they become one with God. When your word agrees with God, they become lord over the situation. God works with His word and brings them to pass when spoken in faith!

The word of God must govern your every utterance. The word of God is a weapon we can use against the onslaughts of the enemy and win. The word of God is the Sword of the Spirit. The word of God on your lips is the key to victory and success. The word of God spoken from your heart releases God to work on your behalf. You don't have to perform it, God will! When a man in faith speaks God's word, those words spoken by man becomes God speaking through man. It is a transference from the spiritual to the natural.

When spoken in alignment with His purpose, God's word on your lips is just as creative and powerful as God's word on His lips. Matthew 10:20, *"For it is not you that speaks, but the Spirit of your Father which speaks in you."* God's word must be programmed into your heart and mouth. When you do that, you program yourself for success and victory. Make your testimony line up with God's word and speak the desired results in faith, and you will see the result you desire come to pass. That is heaven on earth.

I would urge you to lean into the wind and hear His voice. Learn how He speaks and pay attention! The good news is that He wants to speak to you more than you want Him to. Enjoy the journey, the art of hearing His voice. In developing an eternal friendship with God, He delights in making Himself known on every frequency of heaven.

Many voices come from the outside, but His voice often speaks from within and can pierce the heart. It takes God to reveal God to the human spirit. That's why He must live in us.

The Voice Within

I love what Mike Bickle declares in his book, *The Seven Longings of the Human Heart,* "God created every person with deep longings that only He can fill. We all long for beauty, greatness, fascination, and intimacy. We long to be enjoyed, wholehearted, and make a lasting impact. When we realize that these longings are godly, and that God wants to fulfill them, we begin to find new freedom and joy. We are not to repent of these longings but must repent of seeking to satisfy them outside of our relationship with Jesus. To encounter God in these areas is to be fully alive." [vi]

We are in this relationship where Jesus says, the Father's in me, I'm in you, you're in Me. This is dramatic beyond measure! It has the implication that broken human beings like us are allowed to participate in that family dynamic between Father, Son, and Holy Spirit. We are graphed into the family therefore we can be in that Trinitarian conversation. The Lord will fascinate, excite, and exhilarate our spirit with little bits of that. And a little bit of that goes a long way, long way.

In John 14 Jesus is found speaking to His disciples and says, *"If you love me, keep my commands. And I will ask the Father, and he will give you another advocate to help you and be with you forever— the Spirit of truth. The world cannot accept him, because it neither sees him nor knows him. But you know him, for he lives with you and will be in you."* (John 14:15-17 NIV). At first, it may sound like you must earn God's love. That's not what He's saying. He goes on in verse 15 saying, and if you love Me, the second thing I'm going to do is manifest Myself on your heart and your mind in a way that's discernible to you. You're going to have inspired thoughts, not all of them, but more than you've ever had before. You're going to have inspired, energized emotions for me. You will feel my presence and the Holy Spirit will rest on your heart and your mind will be touched. In verse 21, He adds two things to what He already promised in verse 15 to those who love me and obey me. He adds, "If you love me and obey me, my Father will love you." He is promising to come and manifest His presence in you and on you in a way that's discernable to you. It will change your life. You will live your life fascinated with God. If we put those two promises together, He is saying, He who loves Me will be loved by My Father, and I will love him, and I'm going to manifest myself to him.

Let's just isolate that one phrase for a moment because it's so emotional and dramatic; I will hear Him say that He loves me. Imagine one day, you're standing before the Lord Jesus Himself, on that day when you meet Him face to face and there's others around and He looks at you and He looks at them and He points right at you and says, "This one loved Me! This is one who loved Me!" I can't imagine any sentence more powerful than to hear that. And in response He boldly states, "This is my beloved son in whom I am well pleased."

Searching for Fullness

When we come to know the nature of God, but then hear or read something that doesn't sound like that nature, it causes us to search out the matter. We don't ever want to get into deception, but we can't let fear keep us from experiencing all the great things the Holy Spirit wants to show us in the realm of the spirit. We must trust God's ability to keep us, more than live in the fear that holds us back from experiencing the fullness. I like using Google as a search engine when researching or exploring a subject. But the most significant search engine in the universe is the Holy Spirit because the Spirit searches the mind of God and seeks out wisdom. His thoughts were absorbed with you for billions of years in past eternity. You are not a disappointment to Him. Our concept of the Father's loving heart must be clear before we can represent Him properly. I Corinthians 2:9-10 says, *"Eye has not seen, nor ear heard, nor have entered into the heart of man the things which God has prepared for those who love Him. But God has revealed them to us through His Spirit. For the Spirit searches all things, yes, the deep things of God."*

It is true that you only reveal something to someone you love and trust. So, if you love them, they will reveal their thoughts. *"Even so, the thoughts of God no one knows except the Spirit of God. Now we have received, not the spirit of the world, but the Spirit who is from God, so that we may know the things freely given to us by God, which things we also speak, not in words taught by human wisdom, but in those taught by the Spirit, combining spiritual thoughts with spiritual words"* (v. 11-13). And now you speak the language of God, which is the language of the spirit, and when you hear His voice, you understand.

CHAPTER FIVE

Valley of Dead Bones

The Spirit of God took Ezekiel in the spirit to a place of encountering the supernatural vision. Being "in the spirit" indicates He was showing him things in the spiritual realm. It was a dry spiritual valley, an area of a previous war—an arid valley from long ago. A valley always represents the lowest area of your life. It's a dry place, where you feel utterly forsaken. It's a place of death, destruction, and loss. It could be a place of lost things, times gone by from long ago. As we explore the story, God promises that He will bring back all those bones, fitly joined together. He's not going to mix up body parts. Each one must go back to its proper place of origin, and He will reconstruct them with flesh, muscle, and sinew. He's even going to put the faces back on them and then breathe life into them. By giving them His life and making them a multiplied army, He reconstructs a perfectly resurrected army He will command.

This vision symbolized the whole house of Israel that was then in captivity. Like unburied skeletons, the people were in a state of living death, pining away with no end in sight of their judgment. They assumed their hope had disappeared, and they were removed forever. The surviving Israelites felt their optimistic national view had been crushed, and the nation had died in the flames of Babylon's siege with no hope of resurrection. The recovery of dry bones indicated God's design for Israel's future restoration. The vision also revealed that Israel's new life depended on God's power and not the people's circumstances. Putting "breath" by God's Spirit into the bones showed that God would restore them physically and spiritually.

The duality of resurrections mirrors the creative event in Genesis 2:7, describing the creation of Adam. First, God creates the impressively multifaceted human body with everything complete and essentially prepared to work. Second, God breathes His life into us, reminding us how we were made in His image and likeness. God wants to breathe His spirit into all those dead in sin. No other prophet had such surreal experiences as Ezekiel. His vision of the valley of dry bones came to him after God had directed him to prophesy the rebirth of Israel in chapter 36. God announced, through the prophet, that Israel would be restored to her land in blessing under the leadership of "David, My servant [who] shall be king over them" (Ezekiel 37:24), clearly a reference to the future under Jesus Christ the Messiah.

Ezekiel 37:1-3 positions the story of the dry bones. *"The hand of the Lord came upon me and brought me out in the spirit of the Lord and set me down amid a valley and it was full of bones. Then he caused me to pass by them all around and behold; there were very many in the open valley. Indeed, they were very dry, and he said to me, son of man, can these bones live?"* Ezekiel had traveled down those mystical roads before. He knows you don't want to try to out-guess God, so he smartly replies, "Lord, only you would know." That's a very wise answer to use when God asks a question.

Six times 'the hand of the Lord' was mentioned in the book of Ezekiel, usually appearing to indicate something extraordinary and unusual in the prophet's experience was about to happen. This time he was carried visually to the puzzling valley of dry bones. Those bones must have been dead a long time—very old, dried-up bones without any flesh whatsoever. If you've ever driven through the western United States and gone through Death Valley, the lowest point in the North American landscape, perhaps you saw a skeleton that had been there for a hundred years. That's what Ezekiel saw, parched bones.

Can These Bones Live?

When God asks Ezekiel in verse three, "Can these bones live?" so begins the chapter with a fascinating story, the great mystery of the dry bones coming to life. During Israel's seventy years of captivity in Babylon, the darkest part of their history is when this occurred. Israel was outside of its God-given national boundaries. They were taken captive and became enslaved people in Babylon. They were paying a dear price for never taking a sabbath and not letting the land rest for many years. They kept working, disobeying the Lord, and God determined they would go into captivity. They were in captivity for seventy years, one for every year they missed. That's the background to the story.

Here is where it gets interesting. This encounter raises a question. If God was right there with Ezekiel in the process, have you ever wondered why didn't God speak and raise them himself? God shows His prophet, who was a son, this lesson for the mature, the sons, and the overcomers; and He asked him a question. He was about to teach Ezekiel (and us today) a critical lesson. Instead of God showing His power and raising the bodies, He gave Ezekiel an introductory training session in apostolic authority. God put words in the mouth of the one He calls the son of man, an overcomer, and says if you speak on behalf of Me, I'll breathe life into those that have died. In this profound strategy, He reveals how God needed a man who would agree and speak His words for divine purposes. God needs a man with a mouth who can believe what He wants to convey. He needs a man who first believes and then a mouth that speaks in agreement with His words. God revealed a supernatural mystery that would release those called to be a voice that expresses God's word. Then God says, "So again he said to me, prophesy to these bones and say to them, 'O dry bones hear the word of the Lord. Thus, to these dry bones, says the Lord God, *"Surely I will cause breath to enter you, and you shall live. I will put sinews on you and bring flesh upon you, cover you with skin and put breath in you, and you shall live then you shall know that I am the Lord"* ' " (vs. 4-6).

Yahweh's regard for the prophet's answer was equivalent to an admission that the resurgence of the bones lay within His power and not a mere command to predict, as in Ezekiel 6:2 and Ezekiel 11:4. But it was an injunction to speak the Divine word through the miracle of creation, as it should be performed. The significance of the command lies in the fact that it taught the prophet how he would be instrumental in the great work of resurrecting the dry bones. Ezekiel would tell the bones that God would make breath enter the bones, and they would come to life, just as in the creation of man when He breathed life into

Adam, and once again, Ezekiel would know that Yahweh is the Lord (vs. 5, 6).

Life Appears

Ezekiel continues, *"So, I prophesied as I was commanded. And as I prophesied, there was a noise. And suddenly, a rattling and the bones came together, bone to bone. Indeed, as I looked, the sinews and the flesh came upon them, and the skin covered them. But there was no breath in them. And He said also said to me, 'Prophesy to the breath. Prophesy son of man and say to the breath, "Thus says the Lord God, come from the four winds O breath and breathe on these slain that they may live.' So, I prophesied as He commanded me and breath came into them, and they lived and stood upon their feet an exceedingly great army"* (vs. 7-11).

Not having the privilege of a camera, Ezekiel tried to use words to describe the bizarre nature of what his senses experienced. He found it difficult to portray the inexplicable experience — the sounds of rattling bones, the motion of flesh and sinews coming together, and the emotion generated by what God revealed. This extraordinary encounter between the Spirit of the Lord and Ezekiel did not happen in a cemetery, but it may have been a spiritual valley. It's noted here that he was actively pulled up in the spirit to have a panoramic view of what was materializing.

Prophesy to the Wind

In verse nine, God told Ezekiel to say, *'Prophesy to the breath, prophesy, son of man, and say to the breath, 'Thus says the Lord GOD: "Come from the four winds, O breath, and breathe on these slain, that they may live."* We know the wind itself does not intrinsically have any life. It only has oxygen that supports life but is not a life-giving power. The air that blows outside does not have life; only the spirit of God has life. The Greek ruah is the same word as wind used here, and also used in Genesis 3:8, where Adam heard the voice of the Lord in the wind, the cool of the day. The previous verse left the valley full of revitalized, aroused bodies that lacked breath. Now Ezekiel was told to call upon the breath (ruah meaning spirit, wind, and breath), praying the breath/spirit would come on the slain, that they may live. So, God told Ezekiel to prophesy to the wind, prophesy to My spirit, and say, "Thus, saith the Lord." The wind here is the spirit, the breath of God, meaning the man who represents God, speaks on His behalf, prophesying for God. What does that mean? He declares back to God what God already said; God needs a mouth that can agree and deliver God's word back to Him.

As believers, we're all commanded to make disciples. This command has two aspects to it: evangelism (baptizing them) and discipleship (teaching them to observe). The process of discipleship involves making new converts who are baptized, taught His commandments, and encouraged in their growth and sanctification. But where does the power for discipleship come from? We can't convert anybody, and we certainly can't cause someone to grow in spiritual maturity. As a result of the curse of sin, an unbeliever is spiritually dead with no ability to revive himself. How, then, are we to obey the command to make disciples in the midst of apparent hopelessness? This is where Ezekiel's vision of the valley of dry bones illustrates Scripture's teaching about the power of God's Word and Spirit. Making disciples is as miraculous as a pile of bones putting on flesh and coming to life. In salvation and in sanctification, the powerful dynamic of Word and Spirit are the only hope to see dry bones live.

God reveals the reality of the symbolism Ezekiel just experienced when He says, "Son of man, these bones are the people of Israel. They say, 'Our bones are dried up, and all our hope is lost; we are cut off.'" When the scriptures shift from symbols to reality, God reveals to Ezekiel that the breath and the wind were the very heart of the people of Israel who are spiritually dead but shall live again. So, God tells Ezekiel to prophesy to Israel's people, speak in faith, and trust God's word. And God says to Israel: *'I will put my Spirit in you and you will live, and I will settle you in your own land. Then you will know that I the Lord have spoken''* (v. 14).

Son of Man

The term son of man is used diversely in the scriptures. Jesus is referred to as the Son of Man in the New Testament many times, and the term son of man is also found in the Old Testament. Ezekiel is called "son of man" over 90 times. God is God, and Ezekiel is but a "son of man," but finds favor to perform the supernatural by those who love and serve their God. But in Romans 8:19 (ESV), Paul prophetically wrote these words, "The creation waits in eager expectation for the revelation of the sons of God." He changes the term from the son of man to the son of God in the new covenant because of Christ. And Ephesians 4:13 says "until we all attain to the unity of the faith, and of the knowledge of the Son of God, to a mature man, to the measure of the stature which belongs to the fullness of Christ."

When a mature son (this includes women) speaks on behalf of God the Father, creation cannot distinguish the difference between the two. When the prophet spoke to the bones using God's words, they heard the sound of God. The exact frequency is the voice of God Himself. John 1:1 says, *"In the beginning was the Word, and the Word was with God, and the Word was God."* Creation does not hear voices, but it hears the sound of God in the wind. We must recover our identity by knowing we are mature sons of God and overcomers. So, we've got a lot of work to do.

"Then Joshua spoke to the Lord in the day when the Lord delivered up the Amorites before the children of Israel, and he said in the sight of Israel: 'Sun, stand still over Gibeon; And Moon, in the Valley of Aijalon.' So, the sun stood still, and the moon stopped" (Joshua 10:12, 13). Joshua, who was a son, told the sun to stand still. He did not pray to God to come and hold back the sun. Joshua spoke a command that was in agreement with God's words, speaking the desires of God, and creation obeyed him.

The Lord was fighting alongside Israel against the five kings who had attacked them. The picture is quite humorous. Israel is there fighting with swords and spears, while God is in the heavens throwing down hailstones. It says in the story that God killed more of their enemies that day with hailstones than all Israel did with their swords. Now that's a unique way to win a war. At first while reading the story, one might think holding back the sun was done for the army to rest and regain strength. They were getting weary and believed they could win if they had a little more time. So, he commands the sun and moon to delay. The halting of the sun and moon together may have caused an eclipse plunging the land into darkness. This lack of strong sunlight and the confusion caused by the hailstones made it easier for Joshua to defeat his enemies. That is one theory.

But verse 13 clarifies it more with this phrase, *"…until the nation of Israel took vengeance upon their enemies."* As I studied this, it seems quite possible that what happened was that God froze time, froze their enemies in place, and Israel finished the job while the enemies of God stood still and motionless. That's the way God fights His battles. He has many excellent strategies for getting rid of His enemies, which are your enemies. In other cases, God confuses the enemies, and they kill each other. Before this, the armies in Canaan had never fought in a war against an enemy who used supernatural strategies to win as Israel did.

God's Covenant

Joshua's preparations for victory also highlighted the importance of God's covenant. In the opening scene of God's commands, God told Joshua, in verse 6, *"You shall cause this people to inherit the land I swore to their fathers to give them."* This passage alludes to God's covenant with Israel in two ways. First, Israel was not simply to receive Canaan, but to "inherit" it — from the Hebrew verb *nachal.* The land of Canaan is described as Israel's enduring "inheritance" nearly thirty times in the book of Deuteronomy, and more than forty times in the book of Joshua. And second, in this same verse we read that God "swore to their fathers" to give them the land. This refers to Genesis 15 where God made a covenant with Abraham — or "Abram" at that time — to give Canaan to his descendants. God's covenant with Israel's ancestors established that Canaan belonged, by divine covenant, not only to Israel in Joshua's day, but also to the original Israelite audience of the book. And for this reason, they could move forward in their day with strength and courage, just as God had commanded Joshua.

Likewise, the final conquests that are necessary for the perfection of God's kingdom to be established on earth remain ahead. But they have begun, and they were decisively inaugurated in the ministry of Jesus Christ. We get some clue to what the inaugurating assault on the enemies of the kingdom looks like when we consider the text from Isaiah Jesus chose to read and declare while in the synagogue in Nazareth when He launched His earthly ministry. One of the decisive enemies of the kingdom of God are the rulers of darkness and the principalities and powers that do not give up their turf without a fight. Jesus launched a massive assault on them and the New Testament celebrates the intimidation that the greater strength of Jesus Christ created against the powers of darkness.

What this means to believers is that we are no longer under the dominion of fear, fear of evil spirits, fear of death, fear of the control of the bondage to sin. Jesus assaulted all of these things at the inauguration of His ministry. It was then He began dismantling the structures of injustice, deceit, and lies that perpetuate the forces of darkness and their stranglehold on human nature.

The Lord Jesus Christ comes as the second and last Adam. He comes as the Lord Himself, fully God, fully man. He is the one who, in His ministry, brings the kingdom to pass, not only in His teaching and miracles, but establishes the supremacy by His cross, where sin is dealt with. The power of sin and the penalty of sin is removed. It's paid for. Death is defeated, evidenced in His glorious resurrection and ascension and pouring out of the Spirit. The realm of Satan now over us is defeated as we are now transferred from Adam to Christ, from the kingdom of this world to that of the kingdom of God. And in all these ways — through the life, death, resurrection, ascension, the pouring out of the Spirit, the inauguration of the kingdom, which is now here, we await its consummation in the future — He has defeated the powers. He has defeated sin, death, the Evil One, and we are now victorious in Christ.

God's kingdom goes beyond national geographic borders, it goes beyond people groups, and it's a kingdom, as Jesus Himself said, that is "not of this world", and we are not wrestling with flesh and blood, but it's a spiritual battle. The weapons of human warfare are just not appropriate for Christians to use on any level when it comes to expanding God's kingdom. And I think we need to expand that, not just to the actual weapons of warfare, but even our demeanor of "us against them", and we're going to conquer them in some other way.

I think we have every right to dream of that day when the kingdom of God is fulfilled in its entirety, and our experience of life, restored and renewed life, will be what God intended for us. In many ways, the journey back to the completion of God's perfected kingdom is a journey back to Eden, to linking back to what we lost in the Fall and perhaps making it, not only equal to that in a restored way, but better than ever.

CHAPTER SIX

Co-Creators

There is a frequency in the constitution of all creation, of every tangible thing that responds to God's voice. Everything created results from God's divine voice, the synchronicity of God, because nothing is coincidental in God's world. To ask what language God spoke during creation, is absurd. So, what is the meaning of "God said" (amar) during creation? We see its reality in the first three chapters of Genesis, especially in the creation process. But John 1:1-3 paints the missing part of Genesis creation. *"In the beginning was the Word, and the Word was with God, and the Word was God. He was in the beginning with God. All things were made through Him, and without Him, nothing was made that was made."* Nothing was made in a haphazard, disorganized manner without definite purpose and serious intent. All that is made is an intelligent expression of the One who created. The Theos/Logos spoke, but speaking is exhalation.

God exhaled a specific vibration with the frequency of light that created a manifestation of His desired result. There was no one around at that time in which conversation was possible. He didn't need to speak. He just exhaled, and that in itself is miraculous. There's power in His exhale. It's as if God is saying, When I exhale, there's a sound in My voice, in that wind, and creation responds to Me. My creative power is in the wind. The breath carries and delivers My desires and will with a creative force. My creation responds every time that I desire something. Every time He wants to create anything, He exhales, and creation responds because of the creative force within the breath of God.

Son of God, Son of Man

Jesus, the Son of God, became man and spoke on behalf of God, His Father. That's what Jesus did all through the New Testament. He communicated on behalf of his Father and about his Father. So, likewise, when a man becomes spiritually mature, it's a picture of Jesus replicating himself. Created in that image, we carry His likeness. When a spiritual son grows to maturity, he becomes a copy of Jesus, who was the first man of the new creation.

So then, creation itself cannot distinguish the difference in the voice, whether it be the Father or the Son speaking. The voice is an agent of change from a mature son who knows who he speaks for and represents. The Father isn't foolish; He doesn't just allow anybody to carry the full power of His creative words. That would be like handing a child a machine gun and telling him to defend his home. You wouldn't do that because that would result in destruction. He doesn't have the wisdom, the understanding, the knowledge of how to carry out that order safely.

Creation doesn't know the difference between the voice of God talking or the voice of the God-man talking, so long as it carries the creative frequency as the voice of God. When Noah was instructed to gather two of every animal species and place them in the ark, he spoke a word. He gave a commandment, and the animals came to him. He didn't have to roam the earth collecting two of every animal, while trying to round up birds from the air. That would have probably taken another one hundred and twenty years. He had just spent one hundred and twenty years in building and preparing the ark.

God's creation responds to His voice, the sound, and the vibration in the voice. Under direction from the Almighty, Noah only had to send out the call. All creation recognizes the frequency in the voice of the Father. Being in the same image as the Father, the son carries that same voice. I repeated that because we must understand that. That is within the focus of this book.

Partnering with God in the Restorative Process

As a point of illustration, in Ezekiel 37, God told the prophet to prophesy over the valley of dry bones. The Spirit of the Lord was right there in the middle of them and could have spoken Himself but didn't. Instead, He asked his prophet a question which resulted in being

Ezekiel's first lesson in God's school of the prophets. Without knowing it, Ezekiel had enrolled in school and was being trained as to how He wanted a future generation to minister.

God's first instruction was to raise the dead bodies, put flesh back on the bones and create a massive army. Instead of God showing His power all by Himself, how to raise the bones to life as He did before, he enlisted Ezekiel into this dead-raising class. God had given Ezekiel a crucial training lesson when God puts His word into his mouth; creation cannot distinguish who is speaking, the Father or the son. God tells the son of man, (Ezekiel) now prophesy. Your voice carries His power when you are a mature son and know your identity. In other words, you are as I am, so God says I'm going to put the power of My voice in your voice, and now I want you to prophesy and see what happens. That's God's strategy for us today. He demonstrates how we can be His partners doing creative works on earth now!

My friends, marine biologists Francis and Annie MacAulay, were recently exploring off the coast of Catalina Island in California. They discovered that abalone marine snails in a local bay began disappearing and were on the verge of extinction. They took personal responsibility for the restoration and gathered a group of students, teaching them to speak over creation, over the waters, for the abalone shells to come back into a thriving existence. Just as the Lord taught Ezekiel to speak over dry bones, they trained the next generation of students to speak over creation, for it to be restored. Before long, the abalones began to return and slowly prospered and multiplied again. I often think of how powerful their story is and how this principle can be applied anywhere there are mature sons speaking over nature.

As they kept speaking over the water, training their students to speak restoration and purification of the water, suddenly the shells started reappearing. The abalone shells came back and began multiplying. Every year now, they witness the result and reap a harvest; not of abalone shells, but of seeing creation restored by the sound of the voice. They had become the creative force that carried the word of God over creation, and creation responded to it.

In verse 9, Ezekiel's story continues, *"Then he said to me, "Prophesy to the breath; prophesy, son of man, and say to the breath, thus says the Lord GOD: Come from the four winds, O breath, and breathe on these slain, that they may live."* Ezekiel 37:9 (ESV) The word breath here is better translated as wind. In this case, Ezekiel was not prophesying to the air or atmosphere. He spoke to the same wind that hovered over the darkness in Genesis 1:2. He was prophesying to the supernatural spiritual wind that carries the sound of the voice of the Lord on it. That's what God told him to do.

God Put Power in Our Voices

Isaiah 45 tells us God is waiting for a man to command him to prophesy to the wind that he should move. In Isaiah 45:11, God says Ask Me and command Me. *"Thus says the Lord, the Holy One of Israel, and the one who formed him: "Ask me of things to come; will you command me concerning my children and the work of my hands?"* Ask Me of things to come— notice how God talks to the sons, the overcomers. He is not addressing the general believer or the immature Christian. He is not speaking to those who still aren't sure who they are, who are confused and not committed to their identity. Only the sons are confident of their identity because they will recognize the sound of the voice in the wind. They understand authority. He is speaking to mature sons, the ones known in Zion.

Command Me—the scripture implicates Zion as the sons, who are the overcomers. In biblical imagery, "Jerusalem" usually refers to believers in general and includes the young, immature, and not fully grown. But His words of command were for the mature sons who know their identity. God says, Ask Me about the things to come concerning My sons, give Me orders concerning the work of My hands. In other words, He's telling us we're partners in this thing. He says, I want you to work with Me, and we're going to change some things together. I'm adding My authority to your voice on the earth; together, you and I will change atmospheres. You can change situations for the Kingdom to move into a space.

Transforming a Nation in a Day

Let's go a little deeper in understanding the voice of the Lord. Upon writing this, St. Patrick's Day had just occurred, two days before. The following illustration is another example of how a man saved a nation by the word of the Lord in his mouth, transforming a nation in a day. The following is a partial excerpt from the book, Celtic Flames by Kathy Walters. I read it and found it fascinating because it went right along with what I had been studying. I've taken the story, modified it, paraphrased it a little, added to the account, and edited it purely for the sake of congruency. So, it's not a verbatim quote or transcript. It's more like a paraphrase and commentary for illustration.

As St. Patrick came near Dublin, a small village at that time, he stopped and prophesied that this village, which was then very small, would become very eminent. He prophesied, "This little town shall increase and grow in riches and dignity. It shall not cease to grow until it has become the Kingdom's principal seat." In other words, it will be a city with governmental power. He was prophesying over it because He saw what it could become. During that time, the people of Dublin, having heard of Patrick's great signs and miracles, were excited when they saw that he was coming into their village.

At that time, Alphinus was the king of Dublin. They went out to meet him. He and all the citizens were in great sorrow because of the death of the king's two children. The king's only son died suddenly of sickness, and then the king's daughter, a sister to the young prince, had just died because she drowned while bathing in the river known as the Liffey. The name Liffey is derived from an inspirational term based on 'life' and means "the plain of life."

The ritual practices of the druids, who were like mediums, sorcerers, and wizards at that time, dominated most of the culture. According to their superstitions, they had already prepared tombs for these children who had just died. Meanwhile, news spread over the city that St. Patrick was the powerful reviver of many dead persons. He carried a reputation that preceded him, and the people got very excited. How would you like that reputation? Here comes, (fill in your name), the reviver of many dead people? That would be a remarkable testimony in itself. Before you even enter a city, people know your name and come running out to say, "Here comes George, Greg, or Mary. Here is the great miracle worker who raises people from the dead!"

The king had previously rejected the gospel because he and his druid wizards were powerful. So, hearing of Saint Patrick's arrival, the king sent messages and asked him to come into his chambers where his two children were lying dead. When St. Patrick went into the room where the two children were, the king asked him if there was anything he could do in this situation. Patrick replied Yes! There is. Patrick said, If the children rise from the dead, then it would have to be done in the name of Jesus. And secondly, he told the king that if God did this for him, he would have to promise to serve the God of the Christians.

The king agreed before all those present that if God Almighty restored his children to life, he and all those citizens would become Christian. Patrick then raised these princely children back to life, leading to the spiritual resurrection of the king. The result was the turning point of a nation discovering God's original intent. It led to the conversion of all the city dwellers coming into the Kingdom of God. All his subjects were astonished at this great miracle and turned away from worshiping the druid idols. Later, the townspeople were baptized in that same river, Liffey, the river of life. That same day, the king and all the people worshiped God the Creator and gave finances so liberally to St Patrick that he could give to the poor. He also built places for the children to play and began building churches.[vii]

This excellent example of walking in God's power as a son is much like a story right out of the Bible. St. Patrick was an apostle who walked the face of the earth, prophesied, and restored a king's destiny, a city, and a nation in one day. Why can't we do the same?

Hearing the Voice

"For this commandment that I command you today is not too hard for you, neither is it far off. It is not in heaven that you should say, 'Who will ascend to heaven for us and bring it to us, that we may hear it and do it?' Neither is it beyond the sea

that you should say, 'Who will go over the sea for us and bring it to us, that we may hear it and do it?' But the word is very near you. It is in your mouth and your heart so that you can do it" (Deuteronomy 30:11-14, ESV).

This Old Testament reference reminds us that the word of God is not unreachable in heaven. In other words, those in heaven don't hear the word of God; they know the word of God. They know the desires of God. They know His force and power, but they also know His holiness. They don't have to hear the word because they experience the creative breath of the Lord. The angelic hosts experience the sound of the mighty rushing wind.

The book of Revelation gives many descriptions of events in the throne room of heaven. But here, the Word tells us you do not have to ascend to the heavens to hear it; it's available to anybody. You don't have to be unique and gifted in making trips to heaven to listen to the word of the Lord. It's not beyond the far reaches of the oceans where we have to travel to find it. The voice of the Lord is available to us right where we are. *"The word of God is so close to you that it is in your mouth and your heart that you might do it."* (Deuteronomy 30:14) What did that say? "Do it." For a city and its people, for a nation, He did something in cooperation with bringing heaven to earth. It's not that hard to understand. God works through sons. A son not only hears, but he also performs and does things. Sons are doers, and doers are participators. Sons are not sitting on the sidelines; they get in the game and play. They're actively playing the game to win. *"See, I have set before you today life and good, death and evil. If you obey the commandments of the Lord your God that I command you today, by loving the Lord your God, by walking in his ways, and by keeping his commandments and his statutes and his rules, then you shall live and multiply, and the Lord your God will bless you in the land that you are entering to take possession of it"* (Deuteronomy 30:15, 18, ESV).

The writer references restoring the once guarded and prohibited tree of life. When Adam walked away from the tree of life, he took part in the tree of the knowledge of good and evil. It destroyed man's state of perfection. In this reference, God says, I'm setting before you again life and prosperity or death and destruction. You choose. So, we can be partners in this. Zephaniah 3:16 illustrates the point of giving God our command so He can move and act on behalf of us. Zephaniah prophesies what the Lord told him to speak. He says this, *"On that day it shall be said to Jerusalem: 'Fear not, O Zion; let not your hands grow weak.'"* (ESV)

The Aramaic word tzavta, with the same root tzav, means "connection" as well as "to attach" or "to join," and "companionship."[viii] It's God's invitation to please join or agree with Me in this. "Command" is designated for a son. It's not only to hear something being said but implies that you should also "interact in declaring a matter." We read countless times in scripture that God is declaring a matter and then change happens. He teaches us to speak and declare over our situations to bring change. Prophesy to the wind of the spirit and agree with the voice of God because it causes things to manifest. His voice is expressed by agreeing with the desire in His breath, the wind. *"As a man has joy, how good it is by the answer of his mouth, a word spoken in due season"* (Proverbs 15:23). *"For the Lord, the holy one of Israel, and its maker says, "Ask me about the things to come concerning my sons and give me orders concerning the works of my hands"* (Isaiah 45:11). The Hebrew sense indicates to Join with Me, partner with Me, agree with Me, and we will do this together!

The Need for Maturity in an Immature World

Most of my generation grew up honoring our spiritual leaders in a denominational church or some religious order. We were taught to obey the rules, not to have too many questions, and if we use the prayer model of pleading with God like beggars, maybe He will come and do something on our behalf. Maybe you'll get His attention if you beg long enough and whine loud enough. That's sad, but basically, what we were taught. God only tolerates that kind of lifestyle for a while because it's not relationship. He understands this mindset of immature spiritual babies: the naive, the very young children who are immature sons. There comes a time He expects maturity to occur and that His sons actively participate in what He's doing on the earth, those who possess clear identities. They will work with Him to bring changes to the planet. They will initiate change in creation, including the environment, innovations, and atmospheric conditions. We all love miracles, signs, and wonders. We celebrate when blind eyes are opened, and deaf ears begin hearing. We rejoice when the lame start walking. He does that because He loves us and wants us to prosper in health.

The Spiritual and the Natural

In this season, the Lord is directing our attention to the fact that the invisible world is far greater than anything we experience in the natural world. When someone commands a naturally blind eye to open, something from the invisible realm comes and works, doing the miraculous. Heaven is invading earth, bringing God's Kingdom to a localized region. The miracle brings change to a person that can affect a whole city. Today, He is training us like Ezekiel in the supernatural realm of His creative power in the wind of our own voice.

In II Corinthians 4:18, Paul anchors this when he says not to fix our eyes on earthly things; things seen in the temporal world. Instead, focus on the superiority of the supreme, unseen realm, which is greater. We often live in conflict between those two realities. We become distracted by those things we see in the natural, and Paul says we need to focus on the unseen realm because it's more excellent. These two realities are in partnership in a son's life. If they are in conflict, it is because we are still struggling with our identity.

If we look at the imagery of Israel going into the promised land, the Lord promised them that it is a land that flows with milk and honey. In other words, everything's going to be much more significant. You're going to have food, and there is water. You're going to be blessed everywhere you turn. It's a beautiful place that you will own and enjoy. But when they got there, the land was full of giants. They had to see with godly insight. They couldn't look at the natural hindrances. If we look closer at the imagery, this is what God did for them. Israel had much work to do in the natural. They plowed their fields, planted their crops, and then the Lord breathed and blew on their crops. The yields multiplied, and the size of their harvest made it a supernatural harvest. They reaped more than was natural. In this case, the supernatural partnered with the natural realm causing a phenomenal increase. You and I are now the agents that connect the two. It takes mature sons who know their identity and have the power of the Word of God in their breath to bring heaven to earth. By connecting the two realms, we make visible heaven on earth.

Kingdom of God Come Now

In what we call the Lord's Prayer, Jesus taught us this familiar phrase, *"Thy kingdom come; Thy will be done, on earth as in heaven"* (Matthew 6:10). It needs to be the backbone of every prayer that we pray. To have a lasting impact, any prayer you pray starts with this initial framework. Any significant change we've made in life began by aligning our words with the purposes of heaven. In other words, we are prophesying to allow the heavenly realm to overtake this natural realm with a superior kingdom resulting in a divine change. When we study the original phrase in Greek, it becomes apparent it's a command. In English, the phrase is translated more politely. This literal translation is, "Kingdom of God, come! Will of God, here now!" The next time you want to see a situation changed, begin by saying, "Kingdom of God, come! Will of God, here now!" That will transform a place!

Skip Moen, the biblical scholar, said there is little doubt that the Greek text of Matthew reads *eltheto,* which illustrates my point. In a different literal translation, the verse is "Let come the kingdom of You." Eltheto is an active imperative.[ix] That means it is a command – a call to action – not simply an observation. The Literal Emphasis Translation is similar, *"Let come Your kingdom; Let be done Your will."* In the diversity of interpretations, the meaning of Matthew 6:10 is clarified.

At times, being a pastor requires many different functions. I will never forget the time I went to a place of employment upon request of a member of the congregation. She was a single woman and wasn't being treated fairly as an employee. The company she worked for was cheating her out of monthly bonuses simply because they thought they could get away with it. Many years ago, I was in the same type of business, so I knew it quite well. What I did was bring the kingdom of righteousness across the threshold as I stepped across the entry at the front door. I felt very prompted to administer the justice of God in that place. I said, "The Kingdom of God has come to this place now!" While no other human was around to hear that except her, spirits and controlling powers, the invisible world, heard it. It shifted things in the spirit realm. Two weeks later, her situation changed; she recovered all the money the company rightfully owed her and they paid her in full.

We don't have to go in and argue with authority when we walk in greater power. When we take our place as sons, we walk as ambassadors from a different kingdom. We take the correct position of a son with the full authority that God has given. We boldly declare and administer the word of the Lord from a higher power and watch the results. I am not taking a position of bossing God around. I'll double down here and reassure you that we work under His command. He doesn't work for us! Just to make it clear to everyone, we do not replace God. We partner with Him. When we give a command as directed in Zephaniah 3:16, we are to give a declaration that resonates with the same frequency of the voice of God. We agree with what He already has desired and purposed to happen on earth. He's looking for people who come into agreement with what He already determined.

Conversations with a Hindu Priest

During the course of writing this chapter I remembered an incident while on a mission trip to India years ago. This incident happened while speaking to a young priest inside a Hindu Temple. As a group of 27 people on a mission, we felt impressed to go into this Hindu temple to see what God would do. Some people may have trouble with this, perhaps thinking a religious demon will jump on you if you enter a temple of a false god. Being confident we were walking in a higher power, we had nothing to fear which could harm us. Doing this is not recommended unless you know what you're doing and that you are confident of your identity as a son.

Upon entering, we climbed our way up many levels to the main prayer room. That room was reserved only for worshippers. Inside, they had prayers going on, musical instruments playing, and priests doing their stuff. Suddenly an assistant invited us as guests to another special room. In this special room they spoke directly to the Hindu priest and visited with him by invitation only. This room was reserved for unique visitors, dignitaries, governmental leaders, and religious decision-makers. This particular priest was the guy with significant authority over the city. This temple was strategically placed by governing officials on top of a very high hill overlooking the city.

This man was the voice of blessing, cursing, and wisdom in the Hindu world. He acted as a judge, and had a position of power and influence, calling the shots for the city of Bangalore. He was young and spoke more than adequate English, making it possible for us to communicate very clearly. We politely interviewed him at first with many generic questions. What made you decide to be a priest? What happened in your life when you spoke such good English? We found he had a degree in computer science and appeared very intelligent. In time, we got around to discussing more intimate details of Hinduism.

There is a rule in their religious system that says a visitor in their temple is not allowed to mention the name of Jesus unless the priest brings it up first. That's the rule; you are not to mention the name of our Lord Jesus. To do otherwise is risking a jail sentence and they could get rid of you quietly and secretly, and no one would ever know what happened to you. We waited for him to bring up the name of Jesus. As soon as he did, we jumped right on it. As soon as He said, "You call him Jesus or Yeshua; we call him Krishna. It's the same God." We said, "No, we don't think so."

We encouraged him to tell us more about Krishna. He went on this long story about the attributes of Krishna. To make the story short here, he eventually said, "Sometimes we have to take authority over Krishna and spank our god. We do this to make him listen to us and be obedient because he gets out of control occasionally." We said, "We don't spank Jesus because He's the one in control. You know, He might spank us occasionally, but we wouldn't and don't have to spank our God. That alone makes a significant difference between Krishna and Jesus."

Once we finished, they were trying to hand us trinkets as gifts to take home - necklaces, pamphlets, and all this Hindu stuff. We politely said no thank you and got up, almost running out. We weren't taking anything with us from that place and didn't want anything following us home. Objects can carry unwanted entities with them and we were sure to leave them all there.

However, before we left, we did get to pray for him. He was open to that, and his assistant was also. His assistant wound up having a heart murmur. Our friend, Will Hart, was with us and started getting a word of knowledge and said, "There's something wrong with your heart!" At first, the assistant says, "No, I don't have any problem with my heart!" Confident that he heard from the Holy Spirit, Will responded, "Yes, yes! You've had something wrong with your heart for a long time for a long time." Then the assistant finally admitted he was born with a heart murmur. He said, "Well, let me pray for you!" which we all did. Their eyes widened as we left because they weren't sure what had just happened. They had felt a tangible presence of the Holy Spirit that was clean and pure. It was a fantastic time, and we pray it had great long-term results.

God's Delays Are Not God's Denials

God is always looking for bold partners to declare His will over the things of men. Over every misaligned situation, everything that has gone awry in the earth, and everything that has become corrupt, He's looking for a son to restore it to his original intent and purpose. He wants to bring it back into correction. He does that through us, and we bring heaven to earth by partnering with him. God answers every prayer except those that violate our purpose. If we innocently pray something that violates His purpose for us on the earth, He does not answer. We find it recorded in scripture that people prayed and didn't receive an answer immediately. Not because their prayer was out of alignment with heaven's timing and purpose, but only delayed.

An example is when Daniel thought God did not answer him. His answer was delayed 21 days. Then God said, "It's not that I didn't hear your prayer the first time. It was because there was some warfare in between; some things had to be taken care of, and it caused a delay." We get discouraged sometimes when we pray, thinking God didn't answer. We believe that maybe He didn't hear us. But Jesus never taught us what to do with unanswered prayer, did He? Do you realize that He never said, here's what you do when I don't answer your prayer. That's not in the Bible! Do you want to know why He never wrote unanswered prayer into the equation of anything? Because the opposite is true. He is always near, always with us. God says, "I hear your plea. If you speak to that mountain, you can move it!" He never said, "Well, there are a few requests I'm just not going to respond to."

If we encounter a delay, be confident He designed it for you. We are designed to move His heart and bring about His manifest purpose on earth. He wants to invade the earth with His realm of glory. All we must do is lay our heads on the chest of the Father and hear His heartbeat. He gave us a model of how to pray, "Let your Kingdom come, let Your will be done." Both hope and hopelessness are very contagious. You must decide what influence you want on those around you. In the western world, we live in an achievement-centered society where an emphasis is placed on our abilities. In this case, it's our inability that becomes the focus. Instead of emphasizing our inability to hear God's voice, it would be much wiser for us to emphasize His ability to be heard. God makes sure He is heard. We find many examples of this in scripture.

Hearing Disability or Disobedience

What do you do if you are talking to someone who is not listening or has difficulty hearing? You raise the volume of your voice. Can you hear me now? we ask. Then pause for a response. Sometimes we have to look people right in the eye and wait for their attention, as if to say, "You're not hearing me." We take responsibility for being heard. If you're speaking to someone you love, like family or friends, and you must raise your voice to a louder level during the conversation, it might be in protest, but you speak louder because you want to be heard. If we can do this as human beings, God can certainly do this as the Supreme Authority.

It may be the issue is not about our inability to hear as it is our willingness to obey. One of the greatest enemies of our hearts is busyness. Not so much with our schedules, because everybody is busy. Jesus had the fullest schedule of anybody on earth. I believe people following Him, crowds gathering around Him, and people pressing on Him to give answers were a continual activity. He had meals with friends and stayed on the move traveling very slowly from town to town. He also had healing meetings; He had a discipleship training school and was leading an extensive ministry simultaneously. Things got so crazy when Jesus was teaching, people would stay for days to hear Him. They would not have brought food with them, they didn't bring water in their little coolers, nor did they bring lawn chairs for comfort. They were so bewildered and amazed by this excellent teacher that they forgot their daily needs and concerns. If there is anyone who knows what it is to have demands put on him, it was Jesus. However, He maintained a heart of peace. In everything He did, He operated from a place of rest, so He could hear that still, small voice.

God speaks in many ways through circumstances, pictures, dreams, prophecies, and situations. And yes, I like to add that sometimes He even speaks out loud. If we are only waiting for that audible voice, we never seem to get anywhere or start something new. The fact is, He's always speaking to us even when we can't hear. You might have the busiest of all schedules, and it can be very loud and distracting around you, but we must find the quiet place inside us, or we'll miss the still small voice. Proverbs 4:23 says, *"Watch over your heart, for out of it flows the issues of life."* Another translation says, *"Guard your heart with all diligence, for from it flows springs of life"* (BSB).

God is speaking to His sons in this age, and with God's commandment in our mouths, the things on earth will change. God says, Command Me! He is looking for mature sons, co-creators; not just anybody, but those who know Him. A mature son carries the same sound in his voice and releases the word of the Lord into the earth. When we join Him and agree with Him, things on the earth will begin their restoration process. Ezekiel learned to speak to the dead bones on behalf of God. The dead bones responded the same way as they would have to God. The lesson that day was for him to agree with the voice in the wind that word flows from us into creation. Creation doesn't know the difference between who speaks. Was it the Father or the son? Because they carry the same DNA.

CHAPTER SEVEN

God and Time

God takes things that do not exist here and sets them into motion because He already walked through them. He plans it, speaks it, and declares it done. God already made Abraham a father of nations in the eternal realm before he was born into the earthly realm. Jeremiah was the same because He already gave the prophet Jeremiah a job description, a mission, and a calling before he was born. *"Before I formed you in the womb I knew you, and before you were born I consecrated you; I appointed you a prophet to the nations."* (Jeremiah 1:5 ESV).

The Hebrew word for God knew us is yada. Yada here means the Lord knew Jeremiah in a very intimate way. He not only knew him, but He knew Jeremiah enough to instruct him to speak forth His purpose, set destiny, and devise an end goal for him. God knew Jeremiah so well beforehand that He appointed him a prophet to Israel and the nations before he was born. God cared for him, advised him, and put everything in motion before He created him in the natural. I want you to be comfortable knowing God also did this for you. God already knew his character; he could trust this person. The New Living Translation makes the point very clearly in Mark 10:40. *"God has prepared those places for the ones he has chosen."* That's something you could meditate on for a long time.

Matthew notes that the positions of honor which James and John ask for are already designated by God the Father. We have seen how He chose Samson (Judges 13:2–5) and John the Baptist (Luke 1:5–17) before they were born. Jesus specifically chose the twelve to be His disciples, and Paul to be an apostle. The Holy Spirit even chooses who will have what gifts to serve the church. So, as God looks out over all human history with one glance. It's evident that He works directly in that history and invites us to join His work in different ways. We need to focus on listening for His call in our own lives and making sure we answer "yes."

James and John assume that their closeness to Jesus combined with their willingness to sacrifice much and work hard for His kingdom will earn them high positions. This is the way of the world, including the province of Israel. In the church age, honor, importance, and authority do not necessarily go together. Leaders are servants. Unlike many of the kings of Israel and Judah, only those who first honor their wives and lead their families well may lead the church (1 Timothy 3:2–5).

God Sees Differently Than We Do

Upon close inspection while reading the story in 1 Samuel, it is discernible that Saul struggled with his appointed place as king all his life. He struggled with his leadership style and his anointing. People chose Saul to be king because of his great stature and good looks. Saul was tall, dark, and handsome. He stood head and shoulders above everyone else in the room. Good-looking, tall men are sometimes put in places of leadership when they don't qualify. People did not elect him because of his wisdom and character. His physical abilities made him the people's preferred choice. But that's not how God chooses a king. God chose David because he was the most unlikely man to be there. He may have been the smallest, but God equipped him with supernatural power to bring down giants.

John Paul Jackson tells of his experience of the Spirit taking him back in time to the city streets of Jerusalem during the time of David. He got to meet him. John Paul was shocked to discover David to be a relatively short guy. The Bible describes him as ruddy, meaning he was scrawny, yet he defeated every enemy of God. This man had such supernatural power as a mighty warrior. God equipped David with remarkable abilities because He chose him for a specific task.

Never underestimate the power of God and what He's called you to do. You might think you're too small or insignificant, but God declares your purpose, destiny, and function. People believe that a prophet is someone empowered by God to foretell the future.

Undoubtedly, prophets announce God's intentions, but forecasting the future wasn't their primary job description. A prophet's chief task was to serve as God's mouthpiece to His covenant people Israel. The prophet of God would also go to the enemies and prophesy their demise unless they repented.

God Qualifies and Assigns People in His Time

So how does someone become a prophet? Is there some heavenly qualification? Well, there is one. You might think that the standard for recognizing a prophet was whether their words came to pass precisely as they uttered. Accuracy is a standard that we hold people to today. We always say, Well do his words come true? What if a prophet's word is not supposed to happen for 400 years? There is a Bible prophecy that took 1200 years to come to pass. We can't judge somebody's gift and accuracy because of timing. A true prophet's words come to pass precisely as spoken. Fulfillment is a byproduct of the real litmus test. Jeremiah 23:18, ESV, says, *"For who, among them stood in the counsel of the Lord to see and hear his word, or who has paid attention to his word and listened? Who paid attention to his Word and listened? The Lord says, "If they had stood in my counsel, they would have proclaimed my words to my people."*

The real prophet is the one who stands in the counsel of the Lord. The Lord was telling Jeremiah that He knew him before the foundation of the world, had given him a job description, and knew him well enough to trust him. In Jeremiah 1:9, the Lord puts out His hand and touches Jeremiah's mouth and says, "Behold, I have put my words in your mouth." I have already (past tense) put My words in your mouth. Could that be a reference to God doing it before the foundations of the world? God already trusted Jeremiah so much that He already put the words of the Lord in his mouth. We know now that our future is not ahead of us. It is within us. We are not leaving God out of the picture. Your future is not out there somewhere floating in space. If you keep striving, it's not like you'll catch up to it and fulfill it one day. God says your future is already within you. God has committed to what He has already placed in you because it's His own words.

Eternal Beings in a Physical Body

If God knew you from eternity, He's already declared your job assignment and given you the mission. God has already committed to your conclusion; He knows where you're going to wind up because He already walked through it and set it into motion. Everything else that happens to you in this life will pass away. All the hurts, disappointments, and things that went wrong are going to pass away. It's not that He is insensitive; of course, He is very sensitive. What happened in the past is not as important as your future. All the junk in your life will pass away; only what is of Christ will remain. That is the word He has already committed Himself to in your life. We as individuals must become willing participants and cooperate on our part.

Let me explain it this way; you are an eternal being within a limited physical body. You're in a time capsule right now. God has placed you in a body with a beginning and end inside you. In that capsule, you will live out His purpose and destiny. You already have your mission, and your course has been plotted and set in motion. He's committed to you, and it's going to happen. Your future does not depend on your family's bloodline, and it does not depend on what anyone can do for you. It doesn't depend on your adversaries or the giant standing in your way. The Word says in Romans 8:31 that no one can be against you when God is for you! That means you are an overcomer, and your destiny is calling you.

We are usually our own worst enemies. We doubt, worry, fret over small things, and say I can't. We should cease worrying about how long we will live on earth, our health, or how much we have in the bank for retirement; those things are not as important as our eternal life. What if we focus on how effectively and appropriately we are living? Let's be intentional in our life, preparing for the Lord's return.

What is Time?

Have you ever asked yourself, "What is the purpose of time?" Why must I live in time? Who came up with this crazy thing called time?" In most cases, we live by the clock. We go to bed at a specific time and get up at a time; we drive at one specific time to arrive at work on time. We measure birthdays by time, days, months, and years. Sometimes we measure how well we're doing financially by time. As we know it, time is part of the temporal world, and all that will disappear. It'd be better to focus on the spiritual realm of eternity.

Time is the space or separation between events. These events have no direction or particular purpose outside the existence of God. Time has a path, and out of that direction, at some point, meaning arises. Purpose is the ability to form an image of the state of affairs, condition, an end to be attained, or result and respond to that image. I have a sense of purpose, and so do you, because we are alive. Seasons are large chunks of the realm of time. We measure life in seasons. We say, "I'm in a successful season that produces excellent fruit." Some of us are in a season called "the dark night of the soul," but we don't stay there. I may be in a desert right now, but God has a planned promised land in front of me. Ecclesiastes says everything has a purpose of its own within time. Time is defined in the King James Bible as the period between two eternities. There's eternity past and eternity future. Once again, the definition of time is the space or period between two eternities. So, time is an interruption of the eternal realm for a purpose. Six thousand years is just a blip on the radar screen of God, a tiny interruption in the big scheme of things.

Baker's Evangelical Dictionary of Biblical Theology defines times like this: God is transcendent over time.[x] He established the cycle of days and seasons by which time is known and reckoned (Genesis 1:14) and possesses the power to dissolve them according to His eternal purposes (Isaiah 60:19-20); moreover, He controls world history, determining in advance the times set for all nations and bringing them to pass (Daniel 2:21; Acts 17:26). But God is not limited by time (Psalm 90:4). No sense diminishes His person or work: the eternal God does not grow tired or weary (Isaiah 40:28), and His purposes prevail (Proverbs 16:4: Isaiah 46:10).

Even though life is eternal, time is an interruption in all of eternity from where we came. Time is a span of life on earth in which the process fulfills God's purpose. Time causes us to experience and participate in revealing His glory. The universe operates in a specific order to keep time. I like to think of it as an enormous cosmic clock. All planets, moons, sun, stars, everything is revolving and spinning on giant invisible axels and wheels. Every part is running in perfect order indicating a creator designed it. The accuracy alone is astounding, rotating, spinning, and keeping time for humanity to the micro-second.

Experiencing Time Travel

God lives in the eternal realm outside time, and time is contained within Him. He functions in and out of the time realm when He pleases. That's how angels can travel in the spirit and intervene in our domain. On occasion, we too can experience time travel. For instance, how did Philip get from the desert to Azotus? The Spirit of the Lord caught him up (Acts 8:39). After the famous encounter between Philip and the Ethiopian eunuch (Acts 8:26-40), Acts adds a summary statement. After Philip accomplishes his mission, it is noted that he is snatched away and lands in the seacoast town of Azotus. The text reads almost as if the missionary is teleported. *"When they came up out of the water, the Spirit of the Lord snatched Philip away, and the eunuch no longer saw him but went on his way rejoicing. But Philip found himself at Azotus, and as he passed through, he kept preaching the gospel to all the cities until he came to Caesarea"* (Acts 8:39-40, ESV).

Teleportation is the act of instantly moving from one location to another without physically traveling the distance in between. While still theoretical to date, there have been some recent scientific advances in teleporting energy (not matter). But, for now, teleportation is science fiction unless done supernaturally by God Himself. The Bible does not mention teleportation, per se, but it does give at least two examples of miraculous transportation. In John chapter 6:16–21, when Jesus got into the boat after He walked on the water, "immediately the boat reached the shore where they were heading" (verse 21). This is not necessarily an example of teleportation.

The word translated "immediately" does not have to mean "instantly." It could just mean "very quickly." Whatever the case, after Jesus got into the boat, it either was teleported to the shore or was in some other way brought to shore very rapidly. Either way, this amazing miracle is often overlooked. The Spirit miraculously transported Philip from a wilderness between Jerusalem and Gaza (verse 26) to a city about thirty miles away (verse 40). The passage does not say whether this miraculous transportation occurred instantly or took some time.

God is omnipotent and omnipresent. Therefore, teleportation would be within His ability. Whether the two examples above are genuine biblical occurrences of teleportation is unclear. What they do demonstrate is that God is able to supersede the laws of travel and significantly expedite the process. If God desired to teleport someone or something, He could do so. Whether humans will ever be able to invent a device to teleport someone or something remains to be seen.

Another possibility of supernatural translation was when the Lord gave special strength to Elijah the Prophet. He tucked his cloak into his belt and ran ahead of Ahab's chariot all the way to the entrance of Jezreel. (1 Kings 18:46). After using Elijah to defeat the prophets of Baal in a fire from heaven contest, and sending rain in response to the prophet's prayer, the Lord strengthened Elijah to outrun Ahab's chariot. Some have suggested that he ran the 16 miles from Mount Carmel to Jezreel before the king's chariot to honor Ahab as the king of Israel. The lesson to remember here is that the hand of the Lord came upon him to do a supernatural feat. It is not by our own strength that we run. It is not for our own glory that we seek supernatural miracles.

God can unplug His people from the present and transport them to another place in time, backward or forward. He can plug you into the future and give you a glimpse of what He wants to show you. Then He can bring you back and plug you into the present because He lives outside of time. There are no limits because it's all in sync with Him. God is beyond time altogether. God always exists in the now.

God's Manifold Works and Wisdom

"The heavens declare the glory of God, and the sky above proclaims his handiwork. Day to day pours out speech, and night to night reveals knowledge. There is no speech, and there are no words whose voice is not heard. Their voice goes throughout the earth and their words to the end of the world; day by day, they pour out speech" (Psalm 19:1-4, ESV).

"The nights," also by the exact figure, are represented as giving information to each other. In the increasing knowledge already gained, the wonder of the universe displays God's glory, power, and wisdom that we so often take for granted. We have a superficial understanding of this. In Psalm 104:24, David wrote about the discoveries in God's manifold works and wisdom. Would God have just built this beautiful universe with a cosmic clock for us only to look up and admire? No! There is a brilliant design behind it. If people are supposed to know God personally and live according to His will, they need more detailed knowledge than the physical creation can provide. He gave us the cosmic clock, which the Israelites knew as the Mazzaroth, that cannot be changed, lost, or stolen. It foretells the story of the timeline in picture form. He's given us a written word, and He has provided Himself in giving us Jesus as the living word.

Ecclesiastes 3:11 (Amplified) reads like this; *"He has made everything beautiful and appropriate in its time."* He has also planted eternity in the human heart, a sense of divine purpose. There is a mysterious longing that nothing under the sun can satisfy except God. That's a parenthesis in the story. Man cannot find out, comprehend, or grasp what God has done in His overall plan from the beginning to the end. In this verse, "beautiful" means good, goodly, pleasant, well, and fair in its time. In the same way, the term "beautiful" also means "mature and fulfilled in its own time."

God made everything beautiful, and He made it mature and fulfilled in its own time. He made time to bring you into maturity, and He made time to fulfill your purpose and destiny. Ecclesiastes 3:11, NASB, reads, *"He set eternity in their heart."* Why did God set eternity in your heart? Because He knew we would forget living outside of time where we originated. That means God took you out of eternity without taking eternity out of your heart. He took you out of eternity, set you into a place called time, and plugged you in. Isn't that beautiful?

God designed time to cause us to experience and participate in revealing who He is so that we would display His glory. He has made everything beautiful and appropriate in its time. Why did God take you out of eternity and set you into time? That's the number one question people want to understand. The answer is so that He may extend His kingdom out of heaven into the colony of the earth. Scripture says, *"As it is in heaven, let it be on earth!"* He made us His ambassadors in this new colony. If we fail to understand the concept of colonization, it will be impossible to fully grasp the essence of the Bible's message. A colony is a group of immigrants or their descendants who settle in a distant land but remain subject to the parent country. As citizens of Heaven, we inhabit the earth, influencing it with the culture and values of Heaven and bringing it under the government of the King of Heaven. One of God's redemptive values in colonizing earth was to show the spiritual powers of darkness how beings created in His own image could be planted on the earth and bring about the government and culture of Heaven so that the earth would look just like Heaven.

Thank God for Time

Everything God inhabits, He expands. He wanted to expand His kingdom, and the only way He could do that was to send ambassadors to a new place. Consequently, He unplugged you from a place where you're familiar with His heart, sending you into the earthly realm. He didn't send you here alone but gave you His Holy Spirit as a comforter as an accomplice. Secondly, He did that which is good for you. That's why He designed times and seasons. God knew it was good for you, so He created time and seasons for your maturity. And here's another reason: if we were disobedient in eternity like Lucifer or Adam, it would have a lasting, eternal effect on us. We would have remained stuck in eternity as a transgressor. Therefore, God created "time" to relieve us from our eternal bondage. Adam and Eve were expelled from the Garden of Eden for the same reason. If they had eaten of the Tree of Life in their fallen state, they would have remained in that condition forever. Thank God for time! If you fail in eternity, it's an eternal cause. If you were deceived in eternity, it carries an infinite lasting result. Adam and Eve had to enter "time" by leaving the garden for their own sake, so they wouldn't be held in that condition forever.

Almighty God expelled Lucifer from heaven for the same condition. He fell into the eternal realm, and that carries a lasting consequence. He failed in the eternal realm and did not have a redeemable soul because he was not created in God's image. Therefore, being cast out of the holy place was God's only alternative for him. There was no going back. No redemption is available for beings not living in time. Enoch lived in a day where the Watchers came and went from time to eternity. The problem was they disobeyed God by entering improper relationships within the realm of time. Even though Enoch legislated on their behalf, the Watcher angels were judged disobedient and could not return to heaven. In the Book of Enoch, he legislated and pleaded with God to forgive them, but it was impossible. It's not because God is a mean overbearing deity who likes cruelty. Because they lived in the eternal realm, they came from outside of time. According to the laws of that realm, they had to be judged by the eternal standards of that realm.

Time, A Place of New Beginning

Please understand that living in "time" can become a redeeming place. Time gives you a new beginning. We say that time heals all wounds. Feelings of sadness, disappointment, etc., gradually fade as time passes. A woman who loses her husband might think she could never be able to love again, but as the saying goes, time heals all wounds. That is partially true because you can get a new start in time. In time, you can rescue that which is lost. Time can heal, and time can give you a second chance to get it right. The aphorism, "time is a great healer," primarily refers to affairs of the heart; the saying is also relevant to health. Many illnesses respond to the healing effect of time.

God made time to redeem man and heal humanity. God never forces his way. God is simply looking for agreement. You cannot have love if you are not in agreement. Have you ever seen someone try to love somebody who wasn't in agreement with them? They get all crazy. God is looking for people in agreement with Him. He's looking for the nature of heaven within them. God will have an army that responds to Him and walks in agreement with Him without force or coercion. *"Let thy will be done here on earth as it is in heaven"* (Matthew 6:10) agrees that these words reflect that God is love and all He does is good! All He thinks about is your well-being. Sometimes, we lose focus in the middle of our pain and start complaining. It's never true that God enjoys pain. God so loved He gave. God has causative love, not reactive. Causative love has a deep and meaningful objective. God made time to bring about the purpose of all He has placed in humanity. In all of us individually, God looks for those who unite in agreement. He never forces or coerces love. He does not force people to follow Him but looks for voluntary lovers. It never goes well at a dinner table where family members are forced to come. Amos 3:3 askes the question, *"Can two walk together unless they are agreed?"*

God Gave Us Time and a Body

God gave us time to relieve us and rescue us from our eternal state. God took Adam and Eve out of the garden; He took them out of eternity and brought them into time for redemption. He brought them into an earthly place where He gave them a body. I believe the Garden in Eden was not a place on earth as we know it. People have looked for it, and through modern technology and satellite imaging, they found a place where four ancient rivers come together. We can't be sure of its location. It was a spiritual place where they existed in a spirit form. They did not have earthly bodies until after God breathed into them on the seventh day after fashioning them out of clay. As long as you're on the earth, you are here legally. You must have a body and live in it.

Framed within time boundaries, you temporarily live in a body in time. Remember, it's just an interruption in eternity. Demonic spirits always look for bodies to inhabit because they are from the spiritual realm. They are dark spiritual beings that don't belong here. They also need a body to be here legally. If you permit them, they overtake yours. Jesus gave us the power to throw them out because they don't belong here. You are an eternal being having any earthly experience of redemption through time. Your body is your license to be human on earth. You do not have a spirit; you are a spirit. You are a spirit that lives in a body. As soon as you don't have a body, you no longer have the legal right to be here. You must return to God in the eternal realm of spirit. You merely stepped out of time, back to where you came from, where we're all going.

Here's the exciting thing. God gave man the authority to be in a body to rule the earth. God saw that He did not even have the authority to come into this earthly realm without a body. Therefore, Jesus was born as a man because God had to intervene in this crazy place where man messed up. Jesus needed a body to live in while He was here. Jesus became that person, the god-man, the spirit of God living amongst us. He personified the Father. He was not saying, "Let's all take dominion over the earth." He said He created us in the likeness to represent Him on earth with His full authority, speaking His words, decreeing on earth, making it like heaven. He gave us authority, power, and dominion to rule the earth. He couldn't take it back when He issued His Word and gave His decree! God gave His Word, and man reaped dominion and jurisdiction over the earth.

Never Stop Listening to His Voice

I love what Randall Worley once said. Several years ago, he gave an illustration from Genesis 22, where the Father asked Abraham to sacrifice his son. When Isaac was upon the altar, the Lord quickly spoke again before the sword came down and said, "Oh, never mind, you don't have to go through with that!" The Lord was testing Abraham to see what was in his heart. It's not that the Lord didn't already know what was in his heart. He was proving to Abraham what was in his heart. Then He said, "Never mind! Don't go through with that," to let Abraham know. To bring humor to the point, Randall emphasized how happy Isaac was that day to know his father kept listening to the Lord in a progressive manner. He didn't get one instruction and run with it but continued to listen for more along the way.

Can you see the importance of continuing to hear the voice of the Lord? When you think about it, I wonder how many Isaacs have died because they heard what God spoke a long time ago but stopped listening to His present words. How many missions, businesses, and prophetic words died before fulfillment because people failed to hear the current Word?

God's Words Shift Time and Culture

God was speaking a present instruction to them, but they went upon yesterday's revelation. We think we know something because God said it once, so we must go through with the action. Maybe He changed direction because He proved what was in your heart. Suddenly, the sword does not have to come down because the object lesson is complete. Sometimes it's the test, not the mission; that's the objective. It's the present tense voice that is the cause of faith. The nature of faith implies that I am hearing now (present tense). That's where we need to be, in the present tense. Perhaps we need to broaden our perspectives on how God speaks to us.

I'm writing to a mixed audience, so I must cover all this. I know that some of you are very familiar with how God speaks. I hope this book broadens your perspective on how God speaks and that you perceive what He is presently saying. We all have unique experiences, and if I were to ask everyone to tell their understanding of hearing the voice of God, we would all have a different story. We'd all have a fun story to tell, and everyone's would be very different. Everyone's personal story is fun and exciting when we hear so many ways the Lord speaks to us. In each person it's so different.

God will use language that pertains to a generation that He won't use for another generation. From culture to culture, our dreams are different. It is especially significant to say that someone in a particular culture will have a dream that would take on a very different meaning in our Western American world. The implication would be unique because it's specific to that culture. It is custom-designed for each gifting and understanding, down to a personal destiny level. God uses it because He knows that particular culture will understand it. He speaks personally and uniquely to each.

If you heard me speak, perhaps you heard me say that God does not start from a beginning and then work towards an end. He first ends a thing, then starts it, and sets a plan into motion. In other words, He completes a thing before He starts, before He puts it all into action. It's not too complicated for God; it's only difficult for us because we are so linear in our thinking.

Our Beginning Is in God

Isaiah 46:10 in the Amplified says, *"Declaring the end and the result from the beginning and from ancient times the things that are not yet done saying my counsel shall stand and I will do all my pleasure and purpose."* So we, being spirit beings, our beginning is in God. Did anybody begin here on earth? Because you should know that you came from the heart of the Father. I'm going to explain from scripture how God has known us, prepared us, chosen us, loved us, and cared for us, in Him, before the foundation of the world.

When we read God chose us in Himself before the foundation of the world, we must understand that God chose us in Himself. We were in Him, and when God says that He chose us in Him, we had a union, fellowship, common understanding, and prior knowledge of Him. We became intimately acquainted with Him because we were in His heart. God knew us before He created us on the earth. He formed us just like He did with Jeremiah. The Lord revealed this to Jeremiah when he wrote, *"You fashioned me in my mother's womb"* (Jeremiah 1:5). God declares the end from the beginning but always finishes first, then sets a thing into motion. Your life is proof of that, like when the Lord spoke to Abraham, He told him in advance that He had already made him a father to many nations. Abraham was not walking as a father to anyone, let alone many nations. The Lord said, *"I have in times past (eternity past) already declared that you are a father over many nations."* Romans 4:17 says, *"It is written, I have made you a father to many nations in the presence of the God in whom he believed who gives life to the dead and calls into existence the things that do not exist."*

CHAPTER EIGHT

God's Diverse Languages

God's languages are so diverse, they are impossible to count. He communicates through the thousands of languages on earth, and there are many ways in the spirit He speaks. He speaks the language of angels and gives dreams, impressions, prophetic warnings and other intangible ways. We tend to put God on the same level of limitations as humans in understanding, speech, and communication with each other. He often speaks things so profound its way out there for us. It may be way beyond our current paygrade of wisdom and understanding. First, He deposits it in our spirit. Comprehending what He deposited may take days, weeks, or years. That's the only way He can do it. Many have said, "Well, I'm just in a season where I'm not hearing anything right now, but I can feel His presence." Sometimes we are there. His presence is His voice. Why? Because Jesus is the Word, the effect is a voice when the Word shows up.

Humans are naturally a social species. While most of us think we want close connections, we resist vulnerability, the very trait that makes that connection possible. Most of us grew up believing, to varying degrees, that something about us is initially flawed or shameful. As a result, we expect that we won't be accepted and that others will fail us. We try to protect ourselves by keeping our guard up. In a culture that often praises having a thick skin and staying strong and self-contained, we mistakenly brush off being vulnerable as weak. We believe it will unnecessarily expose us to hurts and humiliations we could easily avoid. That is what vulnerability is really about. It is about the willingness to truly be ourselves – to expose a softer side of ourselves that is not hidden behind our defenses. Our world is noisy, with many voices clamoring for our attention, but of all the voices we hear in a day, there is none more critical than hearing the voice of Jesus.

The Christian life is a supernatural one to be lived in a deeply intimate, personal relationship with the living God. Before the fall, Adam and Eve lived in this intimacy and deep unity with the Lord. His Spirit lived in them, and their hearts and minds were united with His. They knew and experienced the beauty and fulfillment of God's love. But, when they chose to listen to the voice of the serpent to be as God, they died spiritually – the Spirit no longer lived in them. Moreover, their hearts and minds no longer were united with those of God. Many today seem to have this disconnect between presence and hearing for the most part. Upon believing and receiving redemption, we heard something in our spirit; and His presence showed up. His voice was there in spirit, as a communication. We didn't interpret it as a voice, and yet it was. We didn't have to interpret the meaning or comprehend it. That came later. Yet, when you got saved, you were responding to a presence. You were having a conversation, and no words were necessary. His presence is the voice of God. It's the voice of God just as straightforward as any voice we've ever heard in life. If there is anything we've ever heard in our life, it's the presence of God because He is the Word.

He is the Word

Standing on the mountain peaks of inspired prophecy, we look back along the highway of history, contemplating with intense awareness how accurately prophecy has been fulfilled. Stretching back in time, the prophet delivered what he thought was a prophetic word but never experienced its reality. Some biblical prophets were discouraged and ran from God, thinking it was an accurate word, but it turned out to look like something else. Maybe they did hear accurately, there was cheating going on, or perhaps a demonic twist was thrown into the mix. But those who read the scriptures accurately will see gaps in fulfilling certain prophetic words. For instance, King David prophesied the crucifixion of Jesus in Psalms 22:16-18. *"They pierced My hands and My feet; I can count all My bones. They look and stare at Me. They divide My garments among them, And for My clothing they cast lots."*

You might be surprised to discover that this prophecy was written 1,000 years before Jesus was born, centuries before the Romans invented crucifixion. How did King David predict the future by saying this would happen to the Jewish Messiah? David was the prophetic voice, and the disciples and others were participants in fulfilling David's words. To understand prophetic predictions, one must discover a more profound sense of tuning in to what the Holy Spirit declares. We were born to overcome impossible situations because God designed us for the impossible, and faith makes the impossible possible. George Mueller, the man of faith, once said, "Faith does not operate in the realm of the possible. There is no glory for God in that which is humanly possible. Faith begins where man's power ends." And we were created to walk in a relationship with God on a journey into the unknown. The following biblical illustration gives us great insight in considering how God includes us in His divine connections.

A Divine Connection between God and Humanity

In Acts 8, Philip and the Ethiopian eunuch experienced a divine connection that fulfilled the plan and promise of God to make disciples of every ethnic group. First, this divine connection began with a clear prompting from God. An angel of the Lord told Philip exactly where to go. Because he was full of wisdom and the Holy Spirit, Philip recognized God's leading. When God tugs us in an unusual way, how do we respond? Secondly, the timing was perfect. The Ethiopian eunuch had questions and God knew exactly how to intersect with an answer by getting Philip to the right place at the right time. When we live recognizing God's sovereignty, we don't give "chance" credit for His work. God always has a strategy. We see the Holy Spirit's leading all through this divine connection. He told Philip to join that specific chariot. What if Philip had paused because the chariot held a foreign dignitary? What if once Philip, a Jew, saw the eunuch was an African man, had pulled back, and questioned the Spirit's leading? God is not confined to work in our boxes and boundaries! We must walk in the Spirit as Philip did, and be watchful and ready when He leads us.

This divine connection was inaugurated by Philip listening. His posture of humility showed a genuine engagement and opened the door for conversation. He heard this man reading Isaiah, and because of the wisdom God had given him, he was ready to connect this wise and sophisticated man to the knowledge of God that he sought after. This was not a brief connection but an extended encounter. The passage says, *"As they were traveling down the road."* According to Levitical law (Deuteronomy 23:1), the eunuch may have been excluded from worshipping at the temple. This precious man had embarked on a long and expensive journey, and now God guided him to read Isaiah 53 where He saw a suffering servant who experienced injustice. Then God brought Philip to share the good news of the Kingdom. We can never underestimate how powerful it is to approach with a listening ear and an open heart.

This divine encounter changed a life. The eunuch was eager to publicly identify with Jesus in baptism with no barrier to displaying his fervent faith. When God's Spirit is moving and leading, we will see His guidance with those He connects us to as well! There was no coincidence that their travel and conversation led them to "some water." God had this whole thing set up!

Jesus loves to confront our weaknesses and brokenness because He is the source of abundance, life, freedom, deliverance, and healing. He doesn't contain the capacity to heal, give life, and secure your release but is the essence of all those things. He helps us confront and overcome our weaknesses because He was the greatest overcomer, and we are created in His likeness. He's given us the power of the resurrection, and it's in our DNA right now to be overcomers and the ability to rise from death.

Paul said in Ephesians 2:6, *"God raised us with Christ and seated us with him in the heavenly realms in Christ Jesus"* (BSB). And hath raised us—the quickening of Christ's resurrection from the dead and our being raised into the life of Christ. And seated us with Him in the heavenly realms—the wonder of being positioned together with Christ in a place of intimacy where the air of heaven is breathed.

Creative Acts Amid Chaotic Emptiness

We must believe we can hear the voice of God even when we don't sense anything. Have you ever sensed you're not feeling anything in the spiritual realm? We are so sophisticatedly designed that it is evident that we have an intelligent creator. Everything with structure has a design, which means a designer initiated it. It takes greater intelligence to be a designer and creator than the design itself. For instance, as an artist, when I paint, the painting doesn't appear on the canvas by itself. Everything starts with a thought and becomes what you see in a vision. I see something in the future of a finished product. Then I begin to paint until something forms on the canvas. I use colors that connect with the shape and the theme of what I saw in that vision that I want to express on the canvas.

Chaos is the opposite of design; it lacks structure or composition. In Genesis 1:2, where the Spirit (ruah) hovered over or gazed upon the earth's waters, everything was in chaos. In other words, it was formless without structure, purpose, or design. There was a mass of something, empty darkness suspended over the waters, but lacked meaning. Picture a dark, void planet without intention and chaos ruling over it. Then God's presence created the light with His breath and took dominion over it, and life grew into the world we live in.

In the book of Psalms, David wrote these words, *"For you created my inward parts. You knit me together in my mother's womb. I praise you because I have been wonderfully made. Your works are wonderful, and I know this very well. In other words, you have been brilliantly made by design and born with a purpose"* (Psalm 139:13, 14, NIV).

The poet David got the picture that there was a designer who formed him. He saw how he was designed for a higher purpose, giving God credit. We are also designed for many great things, but one sure thing for is we can hear from God. It's not as though He is far away. As children, most of us had an understanding that God is way up there somewhere in heaven. We are unsure exactly where, but we think it's somewhere in space. He is only a dimension away. Let's change our thinking and shift into seeing that if we could step out of time, we'd be stepping into another dimension called eternity. That's how far away God is. It's a matter of stepping into another dimension. Do not think in terms of location anymore. Think dimensionally. God is not so far away that we must communicate through satellites or digital signals. But we are comforted by Him when His presence shows up. Sometimes, God expresses love best by not speaking words but allowing us to experience His presence. That is communication as well. Maybe no comments need to be made.

Faith and Hearing God's Voice

We are called to live by faith but desire to hear God's voice. The scriptures clarify that there is a lynchpin between faith and hearing. *"Faith comes by hearing and hearing by the word of God"* (Romans 10:17). Faith does not come from the Bible; faith comes from God through the Holy Spirit. Rhema is the word of God associated with faith; faith comes by hearing and hearing the word of God (rhema). Unless a person hears God's, voice and senses His Spirit when receiving the words from God, there is no rhema, no faith, and no life.

Without faith, you cannot please God, for we walk by faith, trusting God. But it's God's desire and our craving to hear God. Some people simply think that they can't hear from God. Then my answer to them is, "Maybe you're not born again." That's not a judgment. When you responded to God the first time, it's not as though you heard an audible voice saying, "Hey! John, Hey John. It's God here. Please respond. Respond by waving or doing something if you hear Me right now." We didn't say, "Here I am." You responded to an inner prompting when you said "yes" to God. It was pulling on your spirit. There was nudging in the spirit, and you were responding to a person named Truth, who is Jesus. Jesus is Truth. He not only has truth - He is the very essence of truth. So, our conversation was an action in response to He is invitation. We never initiated it. Response to God is always initiated by heaven first. John 6:44 says, *'No one can come to me unless the Father who sent me draws them, and I will raise them at the last day.'*

Hearing God's Word Doesn't Mean You'll Understand It

Comprehension is understanding, but comprehension is not the evidence we've heard from God. We don't have to understand what we've heard to say that we've heard from God. God speaks and communicates in pictures, dreams, mysteries, and visions. Have you ever had a dream, and you knew it was from the Lord? You may not understand that dream instantly. Sometimes it takes days, weeks, months, or years. We obtain understanding sometime after receiving an impression. Prophets can prophesy. They know they heard from God though they may not understand it. *"These are my words that I spoke to you while I was still with you, that everything written about me in the Law of Moses and the Prophets and the Psalms must be fulfilled. Then he opened their minds to understand the scriptures"* (Luke 24:44-45, ESV).

It took one prophecy a thousand years in the Bible to come to pass. The Lord is completely willing to talk to his people and use them to speak His words to others. All it takes is a teachable heart, a mustard seed of faith, and a willingness to step out. God doesn't want to only answer our questions—although those are important; He wants to have a deep, personal relationship with us. Bible study, prayer, and hearing God's voice are all about encountering the Man hidden between the lines.

The Depth of His Voice

In Matthew 4:4, Jesus quoted from the Old Testament: *"Man shall not live by bread alone, but by every word that proceeds from the mouth of God."* We interpret that to mean we can't live by eating bread but by reading and hearing the Word of God. But the meaning is far deeper than that. We live not by bread alone but by every word that proceeds out of the mouth of God. Two primary Greek words are related to words translated in the New Testament as logos and rhema. Logos is the living word, which is Christ. In the beginning, was the Word, and the Word was God (John 1:1). The second primary Greek word is rhema, which refers to spoken word and means any sound produced by the voice. *"It is the Spirit who gives life; the flesh provides no benefit; the words (rhema) that I have spoken to you are spirit, and are life"* (John 6:63, NASB).

Following the meaning of that verse, there are three categories of people. Number one is those who live by bread alone. We can deduct then that number two is those who do not live by bread alone, but every word that proceeded (past tense) out of the mouth of God. That would be those who read the law. Number three is those who do not live by the bread alone but every word that proceeds presently out of the mouth of God.

I want us all to be comfortable and assured knowing that He is still speaking today. We are still receiving life from hearing His words. We are alive because He is speaking. Do you know that you are alive today because God spoke in the past? We live as evidence and testimony of His voice. He spoke the worlds into being; He exhaled the life-giving power of His voice and brought you into existence. That becomes very personal, bringing it down to us being a unique effect of the voice of God, a manifestation of His voice.

God doesn't communicate with us the way we communicate with one another. He communicates from His Spirit to your spirit, and then your spirit communicates what you hear to your mind. That is what we call an inward witness. It is very similar to a thought or a prompting. It's very subtle and requires a closeness with God and regular practice to hear it more quickly and clearly. That's why the more time you spend with the Lord and the more you practice tuning in to His voice, the more it will become a voice that *"thunders in marvelous ways"* (Job 37:5, NIV).

You exist because He spoke you into existence. Romans 10:17 says, *"Faith comes by hearing and hearing by the Word of God."* We often go through that quickly and think, "Oh, faith comes by hearing the Word of God." That's not what it says. It is more accurate to say that faith can only come through hearing the Word of God. We listen to God's present voice to clarify what was written thousands of years ago. It gives us an understanding today. The argument that the Bible is outdated, written so many thousands of years ago, is not relevant today, will never stand. No! God is still speaking, and He's clarifying what He said and is still saying to every generation. He's not adding to it. He's clarifying.

Prayer

Father, I ask that You give us revelation, a more insightful awareness of who we are in You, a vision into our true identity, and the very plan of God concerning our future. Would You give us insight into how You call us to hear and recognize Your voice, open our ears and eyes? Holy Spirit, I ask that You become a revelation in our hearts and that we walk in Your power and true identity every day in Jesus' Mighty name. Amen.

CHAPTER NINE

Truth vs. Facts

Have you ever had somebody ask you, what is God really like? Maybe you've asked yourself that question. Consider the first time God described Himself to a human being. Perhaps He was in a conversation with Moses on Mount Sinai. Moses had just asked, "God, show me Your glory." In the natural you're expecting God to give him some spectacular display of His power and His Majesty or something like that. After all, this is the God who flung the stars into space. The writer of Hebrews tells us that He upholds everything by the word of His power. *"He is the brightness of His glory, the express image of Himself, and upholds all things by the word of His power."* (Hebrews 1:3)

But instead, God does something completely unexpected. God describes to Moses His character. He says in Exodus 33:19, *"I'll make all my goodness pass before you and I'll proclaim the name of the Lord before you."* Then He goes on to say that He is gracious and compassionate. Something immediately stands out here. The glory of God is His character! The reason I say that is the name that appears here in Hebrew is the word Shem. Unlike our English, French, or Spanish names, Hebrew names had specific meaning behind them that was descriptive of who the person was. It would be similar to me saying, "My friend Jack has a good name." In other words, it's not so much about their actual name as it is about the person and character behind the name. So, what is God like? Clearly, He is the sovereign ruler of the universe. God is all powerful and He knows everything. He's everywhere at once because He's spirit. He's eternal, having no end or beginning. He's unparalleled in beauty and majesty. But that's not the aspect of Himself that He wants us to know about Him. He wants to communicate to us that He is a good God, that He's compassionate and He's gracious. And then in Exodus 34, He goes on to describe other attributes about Himself, that He is patient, kind, faithful, and just. That's who our amazing God is. So, why then do we struggle so strongly with the relationship?

If I were to ask, "How are you today?" How are you really? If you're like many people nowadays, an honest answer to that question is probably not "fine." The better and honest answer is "very busy." We live in a culture of scarcity. Many times, we feel like we don't have enough time, like we are lacking something, we don't have enough freedom, money, or talent. It's like we never quit working. We can't do enough. We don't produce enough at work. We don't parent well enough at home, we don't have time for our kids, we're not relevant enough at a church. Underlying all of this is the sense somehow, we're just not enough. We are somehow incomplete and lacking. Psychologists, sociologists and neuro-biologists have studied why sages and poets have mused on this feeling of lack for centuries. Many songs are written about the lack of something.

I believe that wholeheartedness stands at the very center of a son's experience and calling. The difference is where our source originates from. According to Webster, wholeheartedness is an adjective. An adjective is a part of speech that modifies a noun or pronoun. In this case it would be describing you, your heart. Wholeheartedness is defined as: *completely and sincerely devoted, determined, or enthusiastic, marked by complete earnest commitment, free from all reserve or hesitation.* When the devil tempted Eve in the Garden of Eden (Genesis 3:1–7), he stirred up the sinful nature in her. He did this through a clever line of reasoning.

Shame says there's something fundamentally wrong about me and creates a feeling of incompleteness. I lack worth in some area, which means God will not give something to me because I don't deserve it. When we feel like we don't deserve something, we revert to the Tree of the Knowledge of Good and Evil and try to take things by our own strength. We enter the field of self-promotion and make things happen. Remember, we are talking about the same tree that got us kicked out of the garden in the first place. We were thrown out of fellowship with God in the spirit because of self-determination. And now we try to use that same tree to get things back through our own strength.

When the devil tempted Eve, he did not deny that God had spoken. What he did was questioned God's Word (verse 1). He simply questioned whether God had really said what Eve thought he had said. His suggestion was one to make her second guess, doubt, and create unbelief. At the core what he questioned was God's love for Eve. The way Satan asked the questions implies that he was questioning God's love. "If God really loved you, He wouldn't keep something from you, would He?" After the fall, it says they were afraid and ashamed of what they had done. This is still plaguing many believers today.

Shame and unworthiness are the same message from the voice of the serpent in the Tree of Death in the Garden. That voice says, "There is something fundamentally wrong with me." When we become emotionally and physically burned out, we become unhappy in our relationships, with our church, with our children, and those we work with. Things that should not bother us become magnified and a source of irritation. We begin hearing the voice that says, God is not giving me what I wanted and what I deserve. Suddenly we've become the poor victim. Now, I'm sick, lying in bed exhausted, miserable, burnt out, with no emotions, and no goals. We get depressed, we are angry with God, the eternal dialogue says I've poured my life out, I've done all these wonderful things, I got all this stuff, people got blessed, but God did not give me what I really wanted.

One day, God gave me an encounter and I came to an awakening. God began to speak, and it was then I realized, I did all this to myself. Maybe it wasn't God who asked too much of me. I was able to recognize that I did this to myself because I don't feel worthy, I feel like I'm lacking something. If only I could be more perfect like God. That's a hard moment of truth. It is then we realize it's the same voice of the serpent talking. That voice will tell you, there's something fundamentally wrong with you. I am not doing all that I was created to be. I can do more. I can have a bigger ministry if I just work harder. If God won't give it to me, I'll get it by myself! We talk ourselves out of relationship saying, "It's not going to work with You, God - I don't have the faith and patience I need. You are not going to give me what I want. You are too slow, I will do this on my own.

You believe there is something missing. I'm supposed to be in rest, I'm in God's image and yet I've fallen short. I'm working too hard here with no results. It's at this point where we begin to reach with our own hand and take things by our own strength. Now that internal voice says, I will rise above, I will ascend to the position I want, I will get the anointing I want, I will marry the person I want, start the ministry I want. Notice how many I's are in there? All that will only bring death. There is only one fruit on the Tree of the Knowledge of Good and Evil; it's called death.

The fruit on the Tree of the Knowledge of Good and Evil has only one fruit - it's the fruit of good and evil. It's not like the "good fruit" and the "evil fruit," and you get to pick which one you like. No, it's one fruit, the fruit of "good and evil." It's a little good, and it's a little evil, and to taste it causes death on the inside. It's not of God, because the evil causes you to die. Doing good things for God brings death. Doing bad and evil things also brings death, but the cycle is much quicker. Death comes much quicker from doing evil. Doing good, the cycle just takes longer - but the death is still coming around - because it's from the same tree.

Inside the knowledge of "good and evil" is an earthly principle in creation – it is called sowing and reaping. It's going to come around to the guy who says, "This is too hard for me, I'm quitting, I'll go out, do the drugs, I'll sleep around, I'm going to go completely crazy. Then he loses all his money in the gutter like the prodigal son. And then there is the guy who goes to church, tithes his ten percent, does all the things the church needs him to do, and in the end, the fruit is the same, and the person is the same. Why? Both do not know who they are in God's image. Their declaration of God's character, their judgment on God's character and themselves is the same. They've both reached for something - the knowledge of good and evil. The one is doing evil and doesn't know what love is! The one doing good is in the same condition because he doesn't know what love is!

God only cares about what you say about Him. When we read Hebrews 11 (the faith chapter), God is requesting us to consider a rather lengthy list of faithful people. But upon close inspection, they're not good people at all - according to our standards. We make unrighteous judgements about them, while God considers them as heroes of the faith. For example, Moses was a murderer. He's in there. Abraham gave his wife away for adultery. He's in there. David was a killer and an adulterer. He's in there. Rehab was just an outright prostitute, but she helped Israel's spies escape. She's in there. Samson could not hold a secret of God and died prematurely because he had a wicked girlfriend. He's in there. Gideon was weak and frightened. He's in there. Jacob was a deceiver and cheated people many times. He's in there – just to mention a few. That's the facts. But the truth is, God didn't look at them that way. God looked at who they were through His nature, the nature of God. When you look at yourself through the nature of God, you realize that's the only thing that qualifies you to be a son – because you're in His image. By seeing yourself from any other perspective is from the knowledge of good and evil.

When you make a judgment about right and wrong, it might be an accurate judgment - but it's from the wrong system. (Fact, but not truth.) The trouble is - if you're doing good - it brings death where life should be. Because death is the result of the knowledge of Good and Evil. It's good, but it's not God. Good is not perfection. It is not the Tree of Life. There's a difference between the facts and the truth. Facts are death. Truth is life. The knowledge of the truth sets you free, not the knowledge of facts.

You've heard people say, Oh, He's a good Christian. Please call me a son, not a Christian. Why? Christian is a man-given name. There are so many different interpretations of what that means, it's scary. In the past, "Christian" was a name given to us by pagans. Christian is a name given to us by mankind, not God. If you must put me in a category, then I am a Christian. It is a term that describes those who observe and follow Christ. We all understand that and appreciate it. I love the Lord, and I'm happy to be called a Christian in that respect. We understand what it means in common usage, so I am not attacking that. Here is the point: God never created a "Christian" Jesus. Jesus wasn't a Christian. Jesus is the Son of God. Christian is a just a man's term to describe us. But it is based on a judgement from the Tree of Good and Evil. It is a fact, but not the truth.

Jesus is the son of God (that's the truth), I am a son of God because Christ lives in me. His image has been impressed upon me. It's no longer I who live but Christ. Jesus is the uniquely begotten son of God. And we're in that image because He was the last Adam. Jesus was the first creation of a new race. Jesus was the first of many more to follow. Therefore, we are sons with an inheritance, not Christians. Here's why. If you want to be called a Christian, it means you must live up to people's expectations of what a Christian is. If you can attain to this, that's good in their eyes. It's good, that's all. But, if you can't attain what they expect of you, then you are condemned.

Here is the problem; good brings about death. Good is the fruit of the tree that got us thrown out of the Garden. It's good but it brings death. It's the knowledge of good and evil that's the problem. If you can't attain something good, they will condemn you. If you do attain it, you're in pride and God resists the proud. Do you see the dilemma? You lose either way. Jesus is the Son of God and we're in that image. Just call me a son. OK? Now, how many are ready to grow into sonship?

Truth vs Fact

It's the receiving of the goodness of God, the Good News that changes you; not in the changing of you to receive His goodness. When we experience the kindness of the Father's heart, it leads to a changed mind and changed heart. It is not us fixing up and repairing the old nature in ourselves to qualify in being good and then receive His kindness.

The word says, I Cor 15:47-50 *"The first man was from the earth, a man of dust; the second man is from heaven…and as is the man of heaven, so also are those who are of heaven. Just as we have borne the image of the man of dust, we shall also bear the image of the man of heaven. 50 I tell you this, brothers: flesh and blood cannot inherit the kingdom of God, nor does the perishable inherit the imperishable. Behold! I tell you a mystery… we shall all be changed…"*

Do you believe that everything God is going to do for you, He's already done? It's hard for the human mind to receive this, so take it into your spirit. Everything in your mind will fight you on this, but you must take a position, an internal posture – by the spirit - that says; I am perfect and everything else in my life has to rise up to the standard of Christ. Since He is in me and I am the righteousness of God in Christ Jesus, and He's finished the work - then I am complete, I am perfect in Him. If that is true, then I am perfect and everything else in my life is going to have to rise up to that standard. Because here's the other choice…if you don't believe that, it means you're going to have to work at being perfect by your own strength.

If there is work you have to do to become righteous, that means the work of the cross is not finished. That means He is not done with you. That means the blood was and is not complete. That means when He said it's finished, He was not completely finished. But, that's not true. Are you the righteousness of God in Christ? Yes! Are you forgiven? Yes! Are you a new creation? Yes! Now, if you believe you're a sinner - you need to receive Jesus. But if any man be in Christ - you are a new creation. Do you believe that?

Here's what I do. The plumb line is Christ. Everything is measured according to the plumb line. Christ dwells inside me, therefore I am perfect and everything that is not right in my life has to line up to His perfection in me. He, the strength of my perfection, is stronger than any part of my weaknesses. Sitting in the strength of my perfection – is Christ – He is stronger than any of my weaknesses. That means all my weaknesses must submit to my perfection, which is Him.

Let me ask you another question, "What is more powerful truth or fact?" I'll ask it another way. What sets you free, truth or fact? The fact is we're weak. The truth is we're perfect. The fact is we fall short. The truth is I am perfected by Christ. The fact is sometimes I fail. The truth is I've been set free by His blood. The fact is sometimes I might sin. The truth is I've been delivered, washed by the blood of the Lamb. I am the righteousness of God in Christ Jesus. I lack nothing. So, where do I put my trust? In the facts or in the truth?

What sets me free? Knowing the facts or knowing the truth? See Truth as a person. "You shall know the Truth." That means, be acquainted with, shake hands with, know the voice of, recognize the face of, walk with the Truth, a Person of the Trinity, Yeshua. He makes you free. If you are going to put all your efforts, mindsets, thought patterns into the facts about you, and what's wrong with you and what you lack…then you don't really believe the work of Christ is finished.

Jesus ended the Adamic race. That means all that pertains to the fall of Adam, the first Adam, all of his failures, and miseries, all the limited conditions, all the sickness of humanity. He ended it! The problem is that people live by their memory. People live out of their past. People live by facts, but not by the truth. Our minds get in the way. The truth is - we are free! The truth is - we are holy! The truth is - we are righteous. The Truth is within us. The truth is - we are in Christ. I know it's hard for people to receive this.

You know, for years people have been saying, Jesus is coming this year or that year - this month or that month. I'll tell you why even Jesus doesn't know. The son of God doesn't know when He's coming back, only the Father. He will come when there is a glorious, perfect body of Christ to receive Him. A remnant group of sons who are without spot and without wrinkle, who know who they are. I know this is hard to believe because for so long we believed the opposite. We've been taught by religion that we're a bunch of sinners. We've been told by the world we're a bunch of failures. We are complete in Him! We are finished in Him! We are perfect in Him! We're the righteousness of God. In Him, we are holy. We are living in a time like no other!

Never in my entire life have I experienced the continuing degree of challenge we presently face. It's imperative that we know who we are and what we are to do to succeed. I believe this season is partially about coming home to God. In other words, we need to rise to the challenge of the current era. We must know the Father's heart, who we are, and how we are to move forward. I believe God is directing us to focus on engaging the Father's heart and coming to know our identity and purpose. We must come home to who God is and who He has authentically made us to be. I find that most people are not clear about who they are and where they are going. They lack self-awareness. And by lacking self-awareness, they fail to recognize and receive the Father as He is. They will also not perceive who others are in the spirit. I've become weary of the church walking with a dull spirit, unable to correctly discern who they are, stuck in the past, unable to move forward.

The most successful high-level leaders tell us that to be successful requires that we possess the greatest degree of self-awareness. Great leaders know who they are, what their strengths and weaknesses are as well as what their mandate is. Jesus knew who He was and what His mandate was. Paul knew he was called to the Gentiles just as Peter knew he was called to the Jews. John the Baptist became confused during great persecution, losing his identity. Because he lost his identity, he couldn't locate who Jesus was despite being the one who baptized Jesus, identifying Him as the Lamb of God (identity), who came to take away the sin of the world (mandate). As the world becomes increasingly challenging, it's imperative that we know our identity. We must act, diligently seek out, discover who we are and what we are to be about. When we know the Father's heart, our identity becomes much clearer and more visible.

CHAPTER TEN

Between Heaven & Earth

There is a name for the space between heaven and earth, which the Celtic Christians called the "thin places," those rare locales where the distance between heaven and earth seems to collapse. A thin place is either a location or moment in which our sense of the Sacred is more pronounced, where the space between the transcendent and the commonplace is exceptionally narrow. "Thin places" was a phrase used for millennia. The term comes from the mystical world of Celtic spirituality and the Celtic Christians, who were deeply connected to the natural world and considered every aspect of life to be infused with the presence of the Divine, even the ordinary elements of everyday life. Historically the ancient Celts viewed thin places as locations or moments in the cycle of the year where the veil between the world and the spiritual realm diminished and they could encounter those who had gone before them. Today, thin places are more commonly considered locations in which there is an undeniable connection to the Sacred.

A thin place is somewhere you go where you feel God's presence so strongly it's like the atmosphere between earth and heaven is but a vapor. God's presence is so powerful that you feel like He's literally right next to you. Because of these unique experiences happening in these places of encounter, you return to them over and over to experience God there. This is exactly what altars were in the Old Testament. They were places where the men and women of the Old Testament felt like they met God face to face and they built something there as a reminder of God meeting them. The Bible is filled with stories of those thin places where God's presence was uniquely close, like Abraham's account as he traveled through the land as far as Shechem. There he set up camp beside the oak of Moreh. At that time, the area was inhabited by Canaanites. *"Then the Lord appeared to Abram and said, 'I will give this land to your descendants.' And Abram built an altar there and dedicated it to the Lord, who had appeared to him"* (Genesis 12:6-7).

Jacob also experienced this at Bethel, meaning the house of God. For him, it became one of those thin places. Abraham had built one of the first altars and called upon the name of the Lord. After leaving Egypt, Abraham returned to Bethel and prayed to the Lord. Later, when Jacob was fleeing from Esau to go to his uncle at Padam Aram, he stopped at Bethel to spend the night. During the night, heaven and earth collapsed as angels ascended and descended on the ladder with God at the top.

Many years after that, Abraham's wife, Sarah, died. To give her a proper burial, Abraham searched for a plot of land to buy which also included a cave, so he could honorably bury his wife and his relatives. *"Abraham bought the plot of land belonging to Ephron at Machpelah, near Mamre. This included the field itself, the cave that was in it, and all the surrounding trees"* (Genesis 23:17). It's worth noting the last little phrase "and all the surrounding trees." It's one that is easy to pass over as unimportant, but, it is the most important phrase in the whole passage. Why? Because the surrounding trees where the thin places.

How could Abraham buy land without making sure there was a thin place in the near vicinity where he could go and meet with God? In fact, Abraham didn't just buy one oak grove; he bought all the surrounding trees. He wanted to have as many altars as he could to honor God; as many places as possible to position himself for encounter and meet with God in His powerful presence. If there was an ultimate thin place for him, without question it would be Mt. Sinai, the mountain of God where Moses experienced the manifest presence of Yahweh.

The Hidden Place

There is tremendous power in living a hidden spiritual life. It doesn't mean we never venture out to impact the world around us. It simply means we must develop a "secret history" with God in our own secret place. It ultimately leads to having a more significant impact on the world. *"Now it shall come to pass in the latter days that the mountain of the Lord's house shall be established on the top of the mountains and shall be exalted above the hills; and peoples shall flow to it"* (Micah 4:1).

Enoch was Adam's great-great-great-great grandson and Noah's great grandfather, who lived a holy and faithful life to the Lord. He also became the father of Methuselah, the longest-living man. After 365 years on earth, God "takes (him) away" (Genesis 5:24). The verb for "take" appears to mean snatched up or carried away. Perhaps similar to the way God had taken away Elijah the prophet. The Book of Enoch is now celebrated, and much is to be learned about the heavenly realm.

If we want to have a cultural impact and transform a generation, we must lean into pursuing the Lord the way Enoch did. Enoch explains how he spent significant time in seclusion. Enoch 12:1-2 tells us about Enoch being mysteriously hidden. Enoch was hidden, and not one of the children of men knew where he was hidden, where he abided, or what had become of him.

Some of his activities had to do with the Watchers, and his days were with the holy ones. (Enoch 12:1-2) Two things stand out in these verses. First, Enoch was hidden in a physical location to dedicate himself to prayer, where a series of revelations were given to him that translated him to dimensions in the heavenly realm. Jesus also modeled this by withdrawing to deserted places to pray. (Luke 5:16)

The second kind of hiddenness is the reward of our Father, where He positions us in the secret place of the Most-High. (Psalm 91:1) He places us under the cherubim's wings where we are to abide. *"I will meet with you, and I will speak with you from above the mercy seat, from between the two cherubim which are on the ark of the Testimony."* (Exodus 25:22)

The mercy seat is on top of the Ark of Covenant, under the seraphim's wings covering the place where the Spirit of God dwelled. It's a picture of a covenant between God and man. It's a holy place where Jesus presented His spilled blood of the crucifixion to the Father and poured it out as an offering once and for all. Past, present, and future. Our faithfulness to Him is the first kind of hiddenness that opens the door. God's faithfulness is revealed in the second kind of hiddenness.

God Himself rewards us openly before men. Jesus made the concept of prayer simple. He taught us in Matthew 6:6, *"When you pray, go into your room, close the door and pray to your Father, who is unseen. Then your Father, who sees what is done in secret, will reward you."* The concept there is "openly." He will reward you openly, meaning, in front of heaven and earth. So begins your "secret history" with God. The Father's reward for our hidden prayer times is the greatest reward imaginable; communion and intimate friendship with Himself.

Much of the "Sermon on the Mount" (Matthew 6) centers around the secret heart. Everything we pursue in public afterward is brimming with the new life and power flowing out of intimacy with the Father. In other words, the first way to practice "hiddenness in God" is to set a time and place to seek Him privately and often. But those who display their religious activities will not receive any reward. They have already received and achieved their purpose to be seen by men. Since public attention and notoriety are the reasons for their prayers, fasting, and giving, God has no reward to give for these things. The troubling thing is that those who engage in religion to receive the praise of men are not always consciously aware of it but knowledgeable enough to be held accountable.

The Times Are Changing

I don't have to be prophetic to promise that you will experience change from here forward. As discussed earlier, time is the device God put in motion to protect us from remaining unchanged. He has made everything appropriate in its time. He has also set eternity in our hearts. (Ecclesiastes 3:11) We can say, "Well, that was a bad year", or "I lost my job, smashed my car, one of my loved ones died, I had an accident, got divorced, had surgery, and caught that weird Covid-19 thing." Here's the good news. January 1 is the beginning of a new year. We get another chance to make things right. We get a chance to renew our commitments and experience better things. We are given the opportunity to move forward and not be stuck in our old pain and suffering. We can change our surroundings like throwing away outdated clothing that no longer fits.

Change is the only constant in our life - outside of the goodness of God. Change happened during the expulsion of man from the Garden of Eden because God did not want us stuck in that fallen state. He rushed in to save us from eating from the Tree of Life in our fallen state. It would have held us in the clutch of death and corruption for eternity. Change is inevitable within the constraints of time in this earthly realm. Everything around you is set in motion - constantly changing. The air you breathe is changing and flowing.

According to Plato, Heraclitus said that different waters flow for those who step into the same river. Water passes around you and constantly changes if you stand in a river. It's never the same water, and such is your life. Seasons change. The leaves you saw last year on the tree are not the same as this year's foliage. The fruit you picked from the tree this year will not be the same as next year. Snow falls every winter in the north, but it's always new snow. The rain is always unique. It's never the same raindrops from yesterday's rain. Even rain itself causes a change in the properties of the soil it falls on. It turns it into mud. The mud then dries out and changes back to clay or earth.

It is humorously said that the only thing that never changes on earth is a man's mind. There can be no improvement without change. Women constantly change their minds; this is their right; that's what they do. The things we learn by experience are some of life's greatest lessons. We don't have to stay stuck in one place, because another bus of change is always coming in fifteen minutes. Do you want to change? Get on the bus! God is a God of change, even though He never changes. Why? Because He lives in the eternal realm—outside the earthly realm.

Book of Enoch

Time, space, and earth are where man lives right now. These three are part of the same realm. God intervenes in time and space, but He has created that realm for man. The only way He can enter that realm is to become a man, which He did. This is the connection to the Voice in the Wind and walking outside of time where Enoch went to meet with God.

The original Aramaic texts of the book of Enoch have been found in Caves 1, 2, and 4 at Qumran. There is a complete Ethiopic translation and various chapters also exist in Greek, which are used by all modern versions of the Book of Enoch that was published in English in the 1700's. The Apocrypha includes the Book of Enoch. The early church fathers did not include these books in the Bible. They felt that although they may be informative and historical, they were not the inspired Word of the Holy Spirit. But some early church fathers had a more positive view of the Book of Enoch and quoted them often.

There are fourteen books considered Apocrypha, which include 1 and 2 Book of Esdras, 1 and 2 Book of the Maccabees, The Book of Baruch, The Book of Bel and the Dragon, The Book of Judith, The Prayer of Manasseh, The History of Susanna, The Book of Tobit, The Book of Wisdom, and others. Then there is a list of Pseudepigrapha (Greek 'falsely attributed') books that were not written by the original authors, like the books of Adam and Eve and the Apocalypse of Abraham. As Christians, we don't read them like scripture. We read them as historical records that at times help fill in blank parts of biblical history.

In my opinion, Enoch's account is precious because he spent so much time with God that I can only conclude he has a lot of valuable insight and information. Enoch did not experience death because he saw the magnitude of what God would do at the end of the age and longed to be there. He describes this longing in chapter 39; *"After seeing a vision of the houses of holy people, whose intercession is like fresh dew upon the earth, mine eyes saw their dwellings with His righteous angels, and their resting-places with the holy, and mercy were like dew upon the earth."* (vs. 1-5)

Enoch had his very own thin place because he wrote, *"There I wished to dwell, and my spirit longed for that dwelling-place: And there heretofore hath been my portion, For so has it been established concerning me before the Lord of Spirits."* (Enoch 39:8) By using a modern paraphrase, we get a more contemporary reflection of his hunger for God's place of habitation. *"I longed to live there, and my spirit longed for that habitation. And so it became my portion because this is what was established for me in the presence of the Lord."*

In the Book of Enoch, chapter 39, we get a glimpse of what may appear strange at first because Enoch seems to be in two places simultaneously. First, he is swept up into heaven in a whirlwind and gazes on the majesty of God Himself. (Enoch 39:3,6a) However, while there, he sees a clear vision of future events in the homes of the righteous on earth.

Here is the takeaway; we can apply Enoch's longing to both realities he saw in our lives. He longed to remain in God's presence in heaven and to be an active participant in the most significant move of God in human history. This hunger was Enoch's travailing prayer. He did not experience death because God answered his prayer and "established it" for him as a living reality.

Enoch's Time Capsule

Today people study the book of Enoch to find more information regarding the phrase "as in the days of Noah," the Nephilim, or what the earth was like before the flood. However, Enoch's accounts are more than a time capsule from the past—they are a time capsule for the future, providing prophetic clarity for what is about to unfold. Enoch saw our generation prophetically, the challenges we would face, respond to, and what we would become. Then he wrote down his words, and what he saw has been buried in a capsule in the sands of time. Now that we have dug it up and dusted it off, we find that this time capsule was explicitly addressed to us in Enoch 1:2; *"Enoch, a righteous man, whose eyes were opened by God, saw the vision of the Holy One in the heavens, [which] the angels showed me, and from them, I heard everything, and from them, I understood as I saw, but not for this generation, but for a remote one which is for to come."*

But this paraphrase reads more clearly and is more expressive than the Ethiopic version. *"Enoch was a righteous man, God opened his eyes, and he saw this vision of the Holy One in the heavens. The angels revealed it to me, and I heard everything from them, and they gave me clarity as I saw these things, which were not for my generation, but a generation far in the future."* Everything Enoch saw prophetically was meant for a future generation. However, he identifies his target audience even more precisely in Enoch 1:1; *"The words of the blessing of Enoch, wherewith he blessed the elect and righteous, who will be living in the day of tribulation when all the wicked and godless are to be removed."* And again, the original Ethiopic version is not as fluent and meaningful as this paraphrase. *"These are the words of Enoch's blessing, in which he blessed the righteous and the chosen ones, who will live in the time of tribulation, when all the wicked and those who have rejected God will be removed."* (Enoch 1:1)

Enoch's core message is a radical shift from how we think about the end of the world as we know it. He writes his words specifically to bless the "righteous and chosen ones" who will be living in a "time of tribulation." He refers to believers who are living at the end of the age. The Bible refers to it as a time of "great tribulation." (Revelation 7:14) It's essential here that we take note of the small details that make a huge difference. He states, the wicked are removed and the believers, the blessed, the elect and righteous, will be living in that day.

An End Times View Through Enoch's Words

In this verse, Enoch narrows his audience and the timeframe. Traditionally, most of us have been taught that the "end times" and the "great tribulation" are filled with evil, horror, and darkness. Somehow, we get to live through an apocalypse experience only to be tortured and put to death. There is no victory in that. Enoch's words in this passage point us back to the Scriptures, which also identify this period as a time of great blessing, increasing light, and rising glory for those who know God.

He was given a message of hope, of great encouragement. Listen how he explains in his encounter in the thin place; *"While I slept, a great distress entered my heart, and I was weeping with my eyes in a dream. And I could not figure out what this distress might be, nor what might be happening to me. Then two huge men appeared to me, the like of which I had never seen on earth. Their faces were like the shining sun; Their eyes were like burning lamps; From their mouths fire was coming forth; Their clothing was various singing; Their wings were more glistening than gold; Their hands were whiter than snow. And they stood at the head of my bed and called me by my name. Then I awake from my sleep, and saw those men, standing in front of me, in actuality."* (Enoch 2)

To understand how the cloud of witnesses operates, angelic appearances occur, and what happens to us in prophetic experiences, we need to understand who God is and where He dwells. God is eternal and lives in a heavenly realm outside this limited time-space realm. When Enoch prophetically foresaw our times unfold, he was positioned in these eternal realms. It allowed him to foresee our time with greater clarity and accuracy than we do currently. If he could step out of ancient times and into the eternal realms by the Spirit, then he could also step out of the infinite realm and into the end of the age by the Spirit.

Some of Enoch's words suggest that he is actively preaching and imparting something to us from his position in the cloud of witnesses: In Enoch 37:2-4, from the original Ethiopian translation; *"And this is the beginning of the words of wisdom which I lifted up my voice to speak and say to those which dwell on earth: Hear, ye men of old time, and see, ye that come after, the words of the Holy One which I will speak before the Lord of Spirits. It were better to declare (them only) to the men of old time, but even from those that come after we will not withhold the beginning of wisdom."*

Though the above is the original English version of the Ethiopic text, this paraphrase opens the door to a more easy-to-read and stirring translation. *"This is the beginning of the words of wisdom that I spoke when I began to shout to everyone who lives on the earth: Hear, you men of ancient times, and see, you who will come in the future, the words of the Holy One which I will speak in the Presence of the Lord of Spirits. It was easier to declare this to the men who lived in ancient times, but we will not withhold the impartation of wisdom even from those who will come in the future. Until now, this magnitude of wisdom has never been given by the Lord of Spirits, yet I have received based on my ability to see.*" (Enoch 37:2-4) "Lord of Spirits" could also be translated as Lord over all the angels.

It's crucial here that we understand the correct image of angels. Too often we think of angels as soft and feathery; we picture cute cherubic beings who appear on Hallmark cards looking down from clouds like they're having a slumber party. Biblical angels are most often frightening and disturbing. The first angels we meet appear as guards wielding flaming swords as they bar the gate back to Eden. The last angels we meet ride white horses as the armies of heaven. Biblical angels are, first and foremost, warriors who know how to use a sword and who do so with grim effect. Two angels turn the twin cities of Sodom and Gomorrah into a pile of ashes within a day; one angel kills 185,000 of Assyria's finest in one night after their king mocked Israel's God.

The primary biblical image of angels is a military one, and that's how Luke 2 describes them pronouncing peace has come at the birth of Christ. The word "host" comes from the Greek "stratia," a military term literally meaning "army." This was not a choir sweetly singing; in fact, singing isn't mentioned anywhere. On the night of Jesus' birth, with abiding shepherds as witnesses, the heavens are suddenly filled with thousands of rough and ready soldiers of God, an army shouting – not singing – in unison! When God's angel armies recognize a final solution – the way to everlasting peace – when they see it, the moment Christ is born, and His identity revealed, a whole army of angels appears and shouts out a message for all the earth to hear: "Glory to God in the highest! The way to peace has come!" But never in the biblical story – not when Israel carried the sacred ark of God into battle against their archenemies, the Philistines, nor when a young shepherd named David nailed the fearsome giant Goliath with one smooth stone, have heaven's warriors shouted peace or cheered when nations sent armies off to war.

Gateway to Heaven

Today, it does not shock us when an angel appears to someone to give them a clear message or tell them that God is healing someone. The most basic definition of a prophet is that their eyes are opened to see into the unseen realm. We are becoming more prophetic people all the time. Bethel, the house of God, is the gateway to Heaven. Jacob had a dream in which he saw a stairway resting on the earth, reaching heaven, and God's angels ascended and descended on it. (Genesis 28:12) When Jacob awoke from his sleep, he thought, *"Surely the Lord is in this place, and I wasn't even aware of it." He was afraid and said, "How awesome is this place! It is none other than the house of God; this is the gate of heaven."* (vs.16-17, NLT)

The Bible speaks to us about the gates of our eyes, ears, heart and mouth. In the New Testament, it talks about the gateway to heaven and talks about angels ascending and descending on the ladder both for Jacob and for Jesus. There's a lot we need to learn in this generation about spiritual portals. This was a true

spiritual reality then and is so for the present. As believers, we must occupy this realm because if we don't the enemy moves in like he's done for the last several centuries. Presently, we see him interfering in movies, media, and entertainment making it something that it should not be. As believers we need to know who we are and occupy with our identity in Christ. There are multiple spheres of society that as believers we should be on the cutting edge, the forefront, absolutely occupying and setting the standard and presenting the truth of this reality.

Corporate Portals

Jacob saw a blueprint of how the house of God is to function on earth. He saw it as literally an open gateway to access all of heaven. In Hebrew, the word for "gateway" also means "portal." In science fiction movies, we often see portals as "gateways" to other dimensions. Similarly, the house of God is to serve as a portal. It is not a function of the house but of the Lord who has taken up residence. We see the angels of God ascending and descending there because it is a location where the authority to release heaven on earth is made manifest. The house of God functions as a portal because it is the place He chooses for His manifest presence to rest. The nature of God is eternal, omnipresent, omnipotent, and omniscient. In other words, He transcends all of time and space, He is all-powerful, and His knowledge extends infinitely.

The house of God, both you personally and the place of corporate worship, are where He reveals these aspects of His nature to us. Like in Jacob's dream, He releases the full weight of His glory, power, and authority on the earth in a direct encounter. Christ is the gateway and the ladder. *"Very truly I tell you, you will see heaven open, and the angels of God ascending and descending on the Son of Man."* (John 1:51, NIV) When Jesus spoke these words, He alluded to Jacob's dream at Bethel. Christ is the ladder on which the angels of God ascend and descend. The angels who bring healing, restoration, provision, and revelation are released through Him because He redeemed us from the curse.

The Pulpit Commentary supplies added language to the meaning of John 1:51 by saying that the miraculous energies, the Divine revelations, the consummate heavenliness of his life, the power with which his personality moves from the heavenly realm to the earthly sphere— heaven opened, heaven near, heaven accessible, heaven propitious, heaven lavish of love answers the meaning of the mighty words. Likewise, the angels sent to bind demonic principalities and powers and gather the harvest with us are released through the authority Christ purchased with His sprinkled blood. Jesus' broken body is the torn veil through which we have complete and unfettered access to God (see Hebrews 10:20). The separation between God and man was wholly restored through His sacrifice. Upon crucifixion, Jesus declared, "It is finished," as the veil was torn in two from top to bottom. (see Matthew 27)

The separation between man and God is removed in the house of God not only individually but also for a corporate body of believers. It is where the separation between heaven and earth no longer exists, and the glory of heaven pours down into the earthly dimension. Intellectually, we know we have a glorious inheritance and access to all the "mysteries of righteousness" in Jesus Christ. We have a doorway to limitless wisdom and revelation. However, we have yet to access the full glory because we have no idea how.

"Enoch walked with God; then he was no more because God took him away." (Genesis 5:24, NIV) Enoch and Elijah are the only two people God took to heaven without them dying. *"Suddenly a chariot of fire and horses of fire appeared and separated the two of them, and Elijah went up to heaven in a whirlwind."* (2 Kings 2:11, NIV) *"*Enoch was a man who *"walked with God for three hundred years."* (Genesis 5:23) Elijah was perhaps the most powerful of God's prophets in the Old Testament. There are also prophecies of Elijah's return. (Malachi 4:5) *"See, I will send the prophet Elijah to you before that great and dreadful day of the LORD comes."*

Why did God take Enoch and Elijah? The Bible does not explicitly give us the answer. Some speculate that God has prepared them a role in the end times. Others think they are the two witnesses in Revelation 11:3-12. Much speculation is possible, but it's not explicit in the Bible. God may have desired to save Enoch and Elijah from experiencing death due to their great faithfulness in serving and obeying Him. My firm belief is that Enoch escaped death because he chose never to leave a place of revelation. He went from one wild and weighty prophetic thin place experience to the next, which allowed him to move from "glory to glory." The way to become more tenacious in this place of revelation is to spend time there. It takes a lifetime of endurance, faith, flexibility, and tenacity.

Sometimes, there seems to be a "lag time" between the act of seeking and the reward. God is looking to see if we are serious about our pursuit of Him. Jesus explained, *"Ask, and it will be given to you; seek, and you will find; knock, and the door will be opened to you. Everyone who asks receives; the one who seeks finds; and to the one who knocks, the door will be opened."* (see Luke 11:9-10) In the original Greek, these verbs are persistent and ongoing and seek to find. The NLT version reads, *"Keep on asking, and you will receive what you ask for. Keep on seeking, and you will find. Keep on knocking, and the door will be opened to you."* God is actively engaging passionate, persistent, and unrelenting people in their pursuit of Him. Carving out time regularly to seek Him is the first step in the journey.

CHAPTER ELEVEN

The Voice of Many Waters

If you have ever been to Niagara Falls, you'll agree it's breathtaking. With 681,750 gallons of water per second cascading over the central Horseshoe Falls collecting itself tumultuously at its base and creating the sound of "many waters," you can imagine it's overwhelming and noisy simultaneously. Using an oscilloscope to measure sound waves near a waterfall will go off both ends of the meter simultaneously. There is something more profound in the volume of the water falling than our natural ears can hear. There are about 500 other waterfalls in the world that are "taller" than Niagara. The Angel Falls in Venezuela stands at 3,212 ft. but has much less volume. What makes Niagara Falls so impressive is the amount of water flowing over. Most of the tallest falls in the world have very little water flowing over them. The combination of height and volume makes Niagara Falls so breathtaking. But in our spirit, we can be connected and hear God's voice.

"But God has revealed them to us through His Spirit. For the Spirit searches all things, yes, the deep things of God." (1 Corinthians 2:10) There is something about the deep things of God and the voice of God calling out to the deep things in our spirit today. There is a sound He wants us to resonate with, coming out of heaven. It is the equivalent of the sound of a waterfall.Recent scientific discoveries have shed new light on God's voice sounding as many waters. Let's start with the very base unit of our creation: space. Take a cubic foot of any space in the universe, make it a vacuum, and what do you have? Nothing? According to the Bible, every cubic foot of space should contain the Word of God. *"The Word created all things, and all things are held together by the Word."* (Colossians 1:16, 17)

Just a few years ago, scientists thought that space, in a vacuum, contained nothing. They were wrong; empty space is not empty! Now those in science, specifically quantum mechanics, are finding that there is much in this cubic foot of vacuum. They describe it as quantum energy fields that act like waves, constantly moving like waves with ripples. In many ways, they resemble the idea of many waters. It appears that no scientist has yet to associate the quantum vacuum with the voice of God. Someday, they will.

Sound of Many Waters

In Revelation 1:15, John described Jesus' voice as the sound of many waters when he heard Him speak on the island of Patmos. John was undone and fell at Jesus' feet as though dead. But Jesus laid His right hand on John and began to speak. An encounter with God will often begin with the overwhelming sound of a waterfall. The language of Psalms 42 is poetic and metaphorical. *"Deep calls unto deep at the noise of your waterfalls; all Your waves and billows have gone over me."* (Psalm 42:7) I love how the Bible uses this imagery to represent the glory of God. Here again, the sound is deafening. It's not a threatening or intimidating sound, but a glorious one—the voice of God Himself. This calling of deep unto deep, I believe, is to break up our captivity. Whatever waves and billows of affliction go over us at any time, we must call them God's waves, and His billows may encourage us to hope, that though threatened, we shall not be ruined, for the waves and billows are under a divine check. The Lord on high is mightier than the noise of these many waters. After the storm, there will come a calm, and the prospect of this supported Him when deep called unto deep. He calls to the deep places inside us from the deep places inside Himself. He is overwhelming.

If you have ever tumbled in a large wave at the beach it feels disorienting. I discovered this the first time I swam in the Pacific Ocean in southern California. The height and volume of the water creates a force so great, it flips you around and confuses your sense of up and down. The best thing to do is go limp and let it pass over you rather than fight against it. Jesus's voice has much more power than any wave of the sea, carrying much greater force. As the sound of many waters, we may find ourselves, like John, as it were, dead at His feet but ready to listen as we come alive in His voice.

Jesus often comes amid our chaos with a disruptive sound that loosens us from the sound of despair and defeat. Any sound that holds us captive is shattered in His arrival. He steps into our prison, shaking the very foundation with His voice as He opens the door to our soul. On the day of Pentecost, *"And suddenly there came a sound from heaven, as of a mighty rushing wind, and it filled the whole house where they were sitting."* (Acts 2:2) Jesus does come "suddenly" into our troubled and unsuspecting lives.

Why so big a noise? Why not send the Holy Spirit gently, quietly, and without fanfare? No doubt you've heard God is a gentleman, but no, He is a liberator. He's gentle but knows how to make an entrance, command our attention, and distribute His voice. He brings freedom; He brings Jesus! *"And behold, the glory of the God of Israel was coming from the east. His voice was like the sound of many waters, and the earth shone with His glory."* (Ezekiel 43:2) The first time Ezekiel had a vision of God, he was beside the river Chebar. He heard the sound of many waters. He could have dismissed it as the noise of the river thundering along in its bed but didn't. Another time he describes he was not by the river but by the temple, and the sound of water he heard was the sound of God's glory and voice paired together. This same imagery is used in the book of Revelation, where John encounters the risen, glorified Lord Jesus. *"His feet were like burnished bronze, which is made to glow in a furnace, His voice was like the sound of many waters."* (Revelation 1:15) *"And I heard, as it were, the voice of a great multitude, as the sound of many waters and mighty thunderings, saying, 'Alleluia! For the Lord God Omnipotent reigns!'"* (Revelation 19:6) At the marriage supper of the Lamb, the Bride will have a voice of many waters, too. We will have matured into the voice of Jesus.

The Voice That Liberates

So, let's work this backward. In whatever state I may find myself, cast down or disquieted in my soul (Psalm 42:5), I can declare Jesus' victory,

His lovingkindness, His faithfulness, His goodness, and His omnipotent reign. As I do so, there comes a time when His voice speaks louder than mine. When it does, the disruption transforms into freedom. He literally will empower my timid praise with His voice, loud and clear!

After I recover, I will see and hear clearly, and fully understand His glorious work. I am then moved from being shut down, shut up, and shut out into the glorious liberty of Jesus Christ. The Spirit carries me into new heights of revelation and transformation. I am now free. If we are shouting victory at our marriage feast with the Lamb, why not begin practicing now? Since *"God has gone up with a shout"* (Psalm 47:5a), then let us *"clap our hands, all you peoples! Shout to God with the voice of triumph."* (Psalm 47:1) As His voice overtakes you, let go, and let God take you up, higher than your problems, and into His very triumph!

Yeshua was not an example for us, but of us. He was revealing what is possible for all fully mature sons of God. The Hebrew word Elohim means "ruler, judge or godlike one."[xi]   It first refers to Father, Son, and Holy Spirit creating together initially, then refers to you as a co-creator with Him.

Righteousness and Justice

Scripture tells us God's voice is like the sound of many waters. We know from Scripture that righteousness and justice are the foundation of God's throne. *"His voice thundered like a great waterfall. The entire earth reflected His shining glory."* (Ezekiel 43:2, VOICE) *"Your glorious throne rests on a foundation of righteousness and just verdicts. Grace and truth are the attendants who go before you."* (Psalm 89:14 TPT) Putting these two passages together, we see that God's verdicts of righteousness and justice, His words, are the foundation of His throne. They are the seat of His authority and dominion. They flow like a mighty waterfall, filling the earth. *"But let justice flow like a river and righteousness like an ever-flowing stream."* (Amos 5:24 NOG) Like the sound of many waters, His voice is decreeing, in ultimate authority, on your behalf. God's justice is a fierce, mighty, unstoppable torrent that no demon nor hell itself can stand against us! As a fully mature son of God, Yeshua functioned in His role as Elohim, echoing His Father's words of righteous judgment. We see Him in action in Mark 11 when He cursed the fig tree and immediately went to Jerusalem to cleanse the temple, overturning the money changers' tables.

Genesis 3:7 tells us that Adam and Eve sewed fig leaves together and made coverings after disobeying. The fig tree represents the fallen nature of Adam and his attempt to provide a cover for himself. When Jesus cleansed the temple, He dealt with the religious system that did the same thing. These two zealous actions done by God were not random in any way. They were the same: Yeshua, as Elohim, judged the Adamic nature, the religious system of dead works, and the self-righteousness that springs from it. This is why He said to the fig tree, *"Let no one eat fruit from you ever again."* (Mark 11:14) In just a few days, Christ, the spotless Passover Lamb, would end this system forever!

In Christ, your destiny is to create, rule, and judge. You are destined to walk in proper, godly judgment, the fruit of spiritual maturity. *"Everyone who lives on milk is unskilled in the word of righteousness since he is a child. But solid food is for the mature, for those who have their powers of discernment trained by constant practice to distinguish good from evil."* (Hebrews 5:13-14)

The Power of Your Words

We all fail in many areas, but especially with our words. Yet if we can harness the words we say, we are powerful enough to control ourselves in every way. That means our character is mature and fully developed. As you grow to maturity, the outflow of the voice of God through you will enable you to rule and reign, first over your body and then all of creation (James 3:2). When the Father begins teaching us to function as partners with Elohim, He sends the Spirit of Wisdom to teach us the power and importance of our words. *"To fear the Lord is to hate evil. I hate pride and arrogance, the path of evil and corrupt speech."* (Proverbs 8:13) *"By me, kings reign, and rulers decree justice. By me, princes rule, and nobles, all the judges of the earth."* (Proverbs 8:15-16)

At times He asks, "What do you want?" "What do you see?" "What can you dream?" We can change our city through our thoughts, love, and creative words, just as in the beginning. *"You will also decide and decree a thing, and it will be established for you, and the light of God's favor will shine upon your ways."* (Job 22:28)

Remember, because of the cross and the blood of Christ, you are a son of God and a king. A king does not beg and plead; a king makes decrees, and it is done! With that in mind, use affirmations of truth to speak to whatever mountain is standing before you, and watch it fall! *"I say to you, whoever says to this mountain, be lifted and be thrown into the sea, and does not waiver in his lev (heart) but has Emunah that what he says happens, and it will be for him as well."* (Mark 11:23)

The Breath and Wind of God

The fruit of the Spirit, so beautifully developed in the bride, has become a veritable fountain of gardens. Solomon speaks about the pleasantness of a wellspring of God's spirit in you. It's a picture of the bridegroom coming to visit the garden. He's speaking, He's looking at you, and He's given us everything. The garden is a picture of what God is doing in our spiritual life, the bridegroom preparing the bride. It's the imagery of returning to the Garden in Eden where Adam was in the garden. The wind, going forth, carries the sound of God in it.

Verse 12 describes the inner life and heart of the bride: *"she is a garden enclosed, a spring shut up, a fountain sealed."* The well-watered garden of her heart is completely consecrated to her Lord. Verses thirteen and fourteen describe what the Lord grows in this heart garden: the wondrous fruits of the Spirit. Verse fifteen describes the inevitable result of a heart kept and tended by the Holy Spirit "Gardener." Come O winds— Every day is a fresh wind, a breath of God sustaining your life.

2 Samuel 22:11 says, *"He rode upon a cherub, and flew; And He was seen upon the wings of the wind* (ruah, emphasis added)." John 3:8 says *"The wind blows where it wishes, and you hear the sound of it, but do not know where it comes from and where it is going; so is everyone who is born of the Spirit."* And

John 20:22, And when He had said this, He breathed on them and said to them, *"Receive the Holy Spirit."* Whether a magnificent waterfall or gentle whisper, the mysterious sounds and movements are the breathing of the Divine Spirit and the blowing Winds of the Spirit, whose "voice" may be heard and whose effects are present to our senses and consciousness as a living force.

CHAPTER TWELVE

Spirit vs. Soul

Have you ever heard someone say, "I sense the presence of God is here," or "Something about him is just off, or "Something about her being here made me feel uncomfortable?" Maybe the phrase, "Something about it just doesn't sit well with me." We are all familiar with these phrases or phrases similar to them. They all speak of the ability to discern unseen things. Things that are unspoken and generally hidden from our natural mind's ability to see. Spiritual intelligence describes the God-given wisdom of being aware of the spiritual dimension of reality.

The dictionary describes discernment as to the ability to judge well. In the Lexico dictionary, the definition relates to spirituality: *It is the perception in the absence of judgment to obtain spiritual guidance and understanding.* In other words, spiritual discernment is the ability to see, hear, and understand spiritual things that are not readily seen, heard, or understood. It's also crucial for us to establish what discernment is not. Discernment is not an intuition, your gut feeling, or a superpower. It's a spiritual gift given to believers for spiritual purposes.

God's spirit provides spiritual discernment to lead and guide you towards alignment with heavenly objectives and goals. It's an intentional process by God to bring us into cooperation with His plan for our lives. Paul wrote these words concerning spiritual discernment, *"And we speak about these things in words not taught by human wisdom but taught by the Spirit, expressing spiritual* (pneumatika) *truths* (pneumatika in spiritual (pneumatikois) *words. But a natural person does not accept the things of the Spirit of God, for they are foolishness to him; and he cannot understand them because they are spiritually discerned."* (1 Corinthians 2:13, 14, NASB)

Discerning by the Spirit

One crucial distinction in this verse is that spiritual discernment is intricately connected to the Holy Spirit. The gift of discernment comes to our spirit from the Spirit of God. It's not something that comes from being a good judge of character. It's not something that comes from oneself. It comes from God. In Barnes Notes, the theologian wrote that these things are perceived by the aid of the Holy Spirit, enlightening the mind and influencing the heart.

It's a spiritual gift, as the Bible also says in 1 Corinthians 12:10. *"To another the working of miracles, to another prophecy, to another the discerning of spirits, to another different kinds of tongues, to another the interpretation of tongues. God gives us the ability through the Holy Spirit to discern between various spirits and forces in this world."* Spiritual warfare is at the heart of spiritual discernment. As Paul said in Ephesians 6:12, *"We do not wrestle against flesh and blood but against the rulers against the authorities against the cosmic powers over this present darkness against the spiritual forces of evil in heavenly places."*

Whether you believe it or not, there are spiritual forces at work behind the scenes that we cannot see. There are forces of light and darkness trying to influence the human heart either for or against God. The gift of spiritual discernment allows the believer to identify and discern who they are and what those spiritual forces are up to in daily life.

I want you to understand that the gift of spiritual discernment allows you to discern and identify what the spiritual forces are doing, whether good or bad. My point is this; spiritual discernment is a necessary and wonderful gift God gives His people to discern the appropriate response to a situation. Having a spirit of discernment provides a weapon against evil forces. It also helps us cooperate with heavenly beings when they are at work. When "reading the room correctly," we pick up on small things out of God's order. Paul wrote in I Corinthians 2:15 that the one who is spiritual discerns all things.

Understanding Spiritual Things

Apostle Paul has written that only those aided by God's Holy Spirit can understand spiritual things, including God's plan of salvation through faith in the crucified Christ. Others can grasp things intellectually with the natural mind, but that does not mean they can attain spiritual understanding. Some are not discerning the Spirit of truth. There are two major spirits in operation over the whole earth: the spirit of truth and the spirit of error. *"…By this we know the spirit of truth and the spirit of error."* (1 John 4:6) The spirit of truth liberates you from the spirit of error. *"And you shall know the truth, and the truth shall make you free."* (John 8:32) John 16:13 reads, *"But when he, the Spirit of truth, comes, he will guide you into all the truth. He will not speak on his own; he will speak only what he hears, and he will tell you what is yet to come."*

Suppose we can open our eyes and see that our temptations are spiritual, not natural. Then our trials, tribulations, and struggles are spiritual, and the battle for our minds and hearts is also spiritual. It's through the power of the Holy Spirit that we can resist those spiritual forces. Discernment can also mean spiritual insight or appraisal. The Greek word "ankrino" is translated as "to judge" or "appraise."[xii] It is related but not identical to the word Jesus used in Matt 7:1 when He said, *"do not judge."* In this context, the meaning is "to investigate" or "examine."

Paul seems to be saying that a spiritual person is given the ability to see and understand spiritual things and examine everything, meaning spiritual people can assess both the things of the material world known by human wisdom and spiritual things only known with the help of God's Spirit. This gift then causes the spiritual realm to come into sight. You begin appraising what spirits are in operation and influencing the atmosphere in any room.

Spirit and Soul

As God is one as a trinity, so are humans, spirit, soul, and body. *"Now may the God of peace Himself sanctify you entirely; and may your spirit and soul and body be kept complete."* (1 Thessalonians 5:23, NASB) In the outer circle, the 'body' touches the material world through the five senses. The Greek word psyche means soul, heart, and the animating principle that affects life. The soul includes the mind, will, and emotions. The gates of the soul include imagination, conscience, memory, reason, and affections. We have then 'the soul' used generally for the responsible function, in which we live by the Spirit, whose state and movements are expressed in the body's acts, as noted in Matthew 11:29, *"You shall find rest unto your souls."* And in Matthew 16:26, *"… gain the whole world, and lose his own soul? or what shall a man give in exchange for his soul?"* The Greek word pneuma means spirit and is often described as intelligent consciousness. In Mark 14:38, Jesus perceived in his spirit (pneuma). And in John 4:24, pneuma is mentioned twice, referring to God and man. *"God is Spirit (pneuma), and those who worship Him must worship in spirit (pneuma) and truth."* The soul and spirit are much more difficult to separate from each other but can only happen by the Word of God, which is Christ. *"For the word of God is living and powerful, and sharper than any two-edged sword, piercing even to the division of soul and spirit, and of joints and marrow, and is a discerner of the thoughts and intents of the heart."* (Hebrews 4:12)

Certain stimulants trigger or spark the responses of the spirit and soul. These two things are active in your life simultaneously. Our spirit is warring over our choices, and our soul is warring over those choices simultaneously. The battleground lies in that little tiny moment of choice in our stimulus-response. What do I mean by that? A stimulus is triggered when someone cuts you off on the highway. Suddenly, you will be forced to decide, do I yielding to my soul by cutting them off, cursing them, or worse? Or do I surrender my spirit and do what the Holy Spirit says? Each of those, spirit and soul, has a filter, connectivity between the two.

The human spirit requires a 'regeneration' because it was spiritually dead (Ephesians 2:1), and in Ezekiel 36:26-27, you get a new spirit within you by the Holy Spirit. *"I will give you a new heart and put a new spirit within you; I will take the heart of stone out of your flesh and give you a heart of flesh. I will put My Spirit within you and cause you to walk in My statutes, and you will keep My judgments and do them."*

When we live a spiritual life, our spirit becomes the primary filter of our response. It is done by exercising and practicing a spiritual reaction to each situation in life. Then, the chances of having a spiritual response are much more significant. Having a soulish response is much greater when we live life from the soul because it filters out the spirit and lets the issues of the soul become dominant. The solution then becomes, "He cut me off; I'll cut him off or worse." It's the tiny moment between the stimulus and the response, where you cut off the guy or don't cut off the guy – this little moment is called the moment of choice. You either yield to the spirit or the soul at that moment.

The Bible talks about the breath of God, the spirit of God. God fills us with His Spirit, but the question is, does God have a soul? The Bible speaks of God's anger, God's wrath, God's judgment, God's love, etcetera. All of those are emotions that are found in the soul. Consequentially, He must have a soul. We are created in His image and likeness. He is a tripartite being; therefore, we are a tripartite being. He has a soul, so we have a soul.

Does God Have a Soul?

There are supporting biblical passages that indicate God does have a soul. *"I will make My dwelling among you, and My soul will not reject you."* (Leviticus 26:11) *"He could no longer endure the misery of Israel."* (Judges 10:16) Both use the Hebrew word, Nephesh, which means "the seat of emotions and passions, the activity of the mind, will, and character." In Jeremiah 32:41, God promises Israel, *"I will rejoice in doing them good and will assuredly plant them in this land with all my heart and soul."*

We must be careful how we present the idea of God having a soul. We can find many scholars who would argue the point either way. They would say God doesn't have a soul; it is merely an anthropomorphism, applying human qualities to God in a figure of speech. That's why we need a spirit of revelation, not pure intellect. Scripture also refers to God having a hand or a face. It could be that biblical descriptions of God's "soul" are anthropomorphisms similar to descriptions of God's "hands." It depends on how one uses or interprets the term "soul" in context, like when God spoke of being delighted in His beloved son. *"My Servant, whom I have chosen, My beloved, in whom My soul delights."*

(Matthew12:18, BSB) So, when God's soul is well-pleased with someone, He does so with His very self, His essence, His entire being.

So yes, much of this discussion depends upon how one defines the word soul and its context. If we equate the word soul with personhood, then, yes, God has a soul. We know He possesses a mind, will, and emotions that are perfectly whole and sinless. His soul is fully integrated into His spirit and therefore hidden as one. He is a person in that He is a being who possesses a mind, emotion, and will. If we view the word soul as the ability to express emotions, then God has a soul—He is not "soulless" in the sense of having no feeling.

Usually, we use the word soul in the context of humanity. It tells us in the name that the "fall" had to do with the mind, will, and emotions needing to be regenerated through salvation and healing. In the context of humanity, the soul and spirit were one before the fall. They were created perfectly as God's spirit/soul is perfect. The soul became sinful at the fall, and the soul separated from the spirit; otherwise, man would have lived in that fallen state forever. After all, it was a partaking from the Tree of the Knowledge of Good and Evil that caused the effect. The name of the tree gives us clues to the problem. God's spirit/soul relationship is perfect and inseparable and needs no healing or saving. God does everything in patterns, so we can look at those patterns and learn more about who He is.

Soul and Spirit, Tent of Meeting

The spirit comprises three parts, wisdom, communion, and conscience. The soul also consists of the mind, will, and emotion. The body comprises three parts; flesh, bone, and blood. When we understand how all these things interrelate, we recognize that God revealed it in the Old Testament from the very beginning. For instance, one of those revelational insights is found in the Tabernacle of Moses. As we know, God loves to work in threes, like the Tabernacle of Moses is divided into three parts. First is the outer curtain, the tabernacle perimeter, or the outside wall. The second part is the sanctuary, inner court, or Holy Place. And thirdly is the inner part called "The

Mountain of the Lord." It was called that because it was twice as high as the rest of the tabernacle. And, because it was twice as high, you could see it from a long way off.

In Isaiah 2:3, the prophet declared these words, *"Come, let us go up to the mountain of the Lord."* It's as if they said, "Let's meet with God in the tent of meeting. It is a holy place." Isaiah goes on to say that God would teach us His ways. When? When we meet with Him in that sacred place, the mountain of the Lord. It looked like one large tent from the outside, for it was about 30 feet high, 30 feet long, and 15 feet wide. From the outside, it looked like one tent, but you could quickly recognize that two rooms made up that tent when you got inside. It becomes a picture of the spirit and soul.

Many theologians say the soul and spirit look to be the same. From the outside view, they are. But, when you get inside, take a close look, and investigate what the soul and spirit are, it becomes clear that there are two rooms. The picture here shows that the two are part of the same tent. When we are mature spiritual sons, the soul is encased within the spirit, giving the spirit greater power over the soul. The two have separate parameters. The difference is a matter of perspective. If you are looking from the exterior view, you see one tent. Inside the tent, you find two separate rooms, each having its purpose. As a model, the rooms in the tabernacle have different pieces of furniture, each designed for specific functions. So, the two camps may be saying almost the same thing, just splitting hairs.

Seed and the Human Soul

Another difference between soul and spirit is in Jesus' parable about the seed and soil. Consider the likeness of seed and soil to spirit and soul. The condition of the soil directly affects the fruitfulness of the seed. The seed metaphor represents the kingdom, the word of God, finance, giving, salvation, or faith. *"The sower went out to sow seed,"* (Mark 4:3) but in verse fourteen, Jesus said that the sower sows the word. And then, in verse twenty-six, Jesus said, *"The kingdom of God is as if a man should scatter seed on the ground."* One thing remains the same; the seed is never the problem because there is nothing wrong with the seed. The word of God is infallible, which is the seed. The kingdom of God is infallible; salvation is infallible; faith is unfailing. The soil? Well, that's where the problem lies. The soil needed some attention to become useful and productive.

God made us in His image, as it says in Genesis 1:27, and later in Genesis 2:7, we read, *"And God formed the man of dust of the earth, and breathed upon his face the breath of life, and the man became a living soul."* (nephesh) This formation of man from the earth, when God brought forth man from the dust of the ground, breathed into him, made him a living soul. In this case, the soil represents the soul, and since Adam chose knowledge over perfection, the soul became an earthly, natural man who does not accept the things of the Spirit of God. (1 Corinthians 2:14) The Greek word for "natural" is "psychikos," from the Greek word for "soul" and from which we derive our English word "psychology."[xiii] For this reason, it is often translated as the "soulish" the body.

Since the fall of man, there has been a struggle with the soul. The spirit of man is heavenly, causing it to have more significant potential. Humanity was given the choice of two paths; either choose the Tree of Life and remain perfect or choose The Tree of the Knowledge of Good and Evil and live with the consequences. The supernatural work of God is to change the natural man into a spiritual one. By deciding on knowledge, truth is acquired by experiencing God through the redemption process of the soul to become a spiritual one. The soul nature of the woman fell from the state of perfection into imperfection—the man followed his soulish nature. This is not to blame women for anything. We are talking about the soul and spirit.

Mysteries Unfolding, Decisions Being Made

It is a mystery, as Paul states in Romans 16:25 (ESV), *"according to the revelation of the mystery that was kept secret for long ages,"* and in 1 Corinthians 2:7, (BSB) *"we speak of the mysterious and hidden wisdom of God, which He destined for our glory before time began."* Ephesians 3:9, *"to make all see what is the fellowship of the mystery, which from the beginning of the ages has been hidden in God."* Colossians 1:26, *"the mystery which has been hidden from ages and from generations, but now has been revealed to the saints."* As used here, a definition for mystery is "a hidden purpose or counsel, or secret will." The secret purposes of God's kingdom and will are hidden from ungodly mortals but revealed to righteous men as He chooses. When we recognize two separate rooms in that tabernacle sanctuary, we also realize that there are two rooms within our heart's sanctuary within our being.

There's a room for the spirit, representing the Holy of Holies, where God makes Himself known to us and rests inside us. Jesus said, *"If anyone loves Me, he will follow My word; and My Father will love him, and We will come to him and make Our dwelling with him."* (John 14:23, NASB) I can imagine God saying, "That's where that dwelling takes place, in the Holy of Holies." And there is a room for the soul; that's where your mind, will, and emotions rest. But that's where the war takes place that Paul talks about when he writes, *"I see in my members another law waging war against the law of my mind and making me captive to the law of sin that dwells in my members."* (Romans 7:23)

What member of your soul is ruling your responses? Do your mind or emotions rule, or does your spirit have dominion? Maybe it's your will that rules, or perhaps the wisdom in your spirit rules your decisions. Does your communion with God lead with your conscience? The answers to these questions are essential because it indicates how you hear from God through the Holy Spirit. When the Holy Spirit says, "Don't go here, go over here. Stop! Watch this, don't go into that building, pay attention to what you're looking at", etc. Simply put, the filters of Spirit and soul prompt response to each situation or stimulation. Both God and the enemy are looking for a response to everything we encounter. We encounter numerous stimuli throughout the day with every event.

We have a choice as to how we will respond to that event. These ingredients, the stimulus, the moment of choice, and our response, become the primary deciding factor that will either help you hear from

God continually or keep you from hearing God continually. These patterns in the habit of response we create are the components that shape and express our character. *"Sow a thought; you reap an action; sow an act, you reap a habit; sow a habit, you reap a character; sow a character, you reap a destiny."* (Ralph Waldo Emerson)

I want all of us to cultivate a habit of response that activates a spiritual filter, so we respond maturely in any given situation. Our response habits affect how we hear and respond to God, which affects our ability to discern the voice in the wind. When our spirit rules us, our will responds with the fruit of the Spirit. Conversely, our choices produce a soulish, harmful and destructive response when our soul leads us. We are personally responsible for how we respond. In the long term, it becomes our character.

Yahweh's House

When we recognize that there were two rooms in the sanctuary of the tabernacle, we also understand that in the sanctuary of our heart there are two rooms as well. There's a room for the spirit, the Holy of Holies. It is where God makes himself known to us and where God rests inside of us. We have become the ark of the covenant under the New Covenant. Jesus said, *"My father and I will come and dwell with you."* That's where that dwelling takes place. Jesus said, in John 14:2, *"In my Father's house are many mansions: if it were not so, I would have told you. I go to prepare a place for you."* The mansions Yeshua mentions are rooms in a house, Yahweh's house. I believe we have a house and rooms in our house. The house is our mind, a space where the furniture of heaven is meant to be placed. These rooms, the spirit and soul, are intended to be filled with the light and glory of Christ alone.

The wind of the Spirit blows mightily through these rooms, creating sounds that are discerned in the spirit. These rooms of our mind are throne rooms. These rooms are often occupied by illegal words, thoughts, and strongholds, which are imposters. They have taken up residence there by influential curses. When salvation occurs, the wind of the Holy Spirit begins blowing through this incredible place, then the sounds of heaven begin to resonate. There is a result in renewing the spirit of your mind. What is that? The spirit of your mind? That's another fascinating subject for another day.

War of the Soul and Torn Veil

Looking into the soul is where your emotions lie. That's where the war is happening. Paul writes, *"I war within myself regarding what to do."* Two New Testament scriptures give us a clear understanding of this. I hope it is easier to ascertain now that we have a moment of clarity where there is a soul and spirit. The two are separate but can be one. Hebrews 4:12 talks about the Word of God is sharper than any two-edged sword piercing and dividing between the soul and the spirit. There would be no need to write that verse if there were only spirits without a soul. It says the Word divides between the soul and the spirit. There is a clear distinction between the two.

The phrase "sharper than a two-edged sword" was illustrated when the veil tore in the Holy Place on Jesus' crucifixion day. The Holy of Holies was separated from the Holy Place. When Jesus was slain on the cross, the first thing that happened was the veil was ripped from top to bottom. It started in the heavenly realm and came down to the earth, thus saying that He gave us free access to the presence of God. This was symbolically saying the flesh was the veil and had just been crucified. That moment represented a putting-back-together moment of the spirit and soul. Fellowship between the spirit and soul was just restored. As a sign, the literal veil in the tabernacle was ripped apart.

The Blameless Soul

God Himself is doing something within you, and that something is the sanctification of your soul and spirit. The sanctification includes these three parts. *"Now may the God of Peace, Himself, sanctify you completely, and may your whole spirit, soul, and body be preserved blameless at the coming of our Lord."* (1 Thessalonians 5:23) The Greek word "amemptos" means blameless, faultless, free from fault or defect, or not finding fault.[xiv]

After examining the words, it is clear God envisioned the conclusion. To reach that glorious moment, God sanctifies His people by the Spirit of God, making them holy and perfect, meaning reaching the place of their original state in Eden. It seems that Paul's prayer is that the work of the Holy Spirit in the lives of the saints will be preserved.

It is not enough to encounter that original experience of the Spirit but to maintain the work accomplished while remaining blameless. In John Gill's notes, who is highly respected by all, he wrote these words related to 1 Thessalonians 5:23. *Preserved blameless—"be kept from a total and final falling away, the work of grace be at last completed on the soul and spirit, and the body be raised in incorruption, and glory; and both at the coming of Christ be presented faultless, and without blame, without spot or wrinkle, or any such thing, first to himself, and then to his Father."*

Paul is saying that to remain blameless is possible, a point where your whole being is sanctified and becomes blameless. The totality of who we are is wholly sanctified, that we are no longer corrupt. It becomes clear that Paul wrote these three things because of his concern to be preserved blameless at the coming of the Lord.

There's value in saying that we need to search out that spiritual reality, determining what it looks like to have a blameless spirit. What does an innocent sanctified soul look like? How does the blameless body appear to be? These two passages are apparent, indicating the distinct difference between body, soul, and spirit. But the actual battleground lies with the spirit/soul relationship *"And to be made new in the attitude of your minds; and to put on the new self, created to be like God in true righteousness and holiness."* (Ephesians 4:23-24, NIV)

When our spirit and soul are complete, our bodies will do what they are told, but our soulish parts (including our intellect) are responsible for choosing or exercising our free will. So, in that sense, a person's soul has master control over their whole person. For the born-again person, the spirit is the driving, life-giving force, but the soul has the last say because it houses the mind, will, and emotions. God will not violate our free will except in final judgment. Without going into any complex theology, I believe two critical things. First, the soul needs "saving" and healing. Our carnal nature, our sin-sick soul, displays what we are without the spirit of Christ in us, the hope of glory.

Secondly and primarily, we experience God through our spirit. We can feel God's presence in our soul, but God is spirit and communes with us through our spirit, which is different from our soul. They can either work together or against each other. The spirit is always considered masculine in gender. The nature of the soul is feminine in gender. That is why Eve had to sin first; it was the soul of man that failed first, not the spirit. Nothing against women – I am not blaming women. Is that clear? It's figurative because the masculine failed too.

The spirit followed the leading of the soul. *"Husbands, in the same way, live with your wives with an understanding of their weaker nature, yet showing them honor as coheirs of the grace of life, so that your prayers will not be hindered."* (I Peter 3:7) Peter is telling us that the soul is weaker than the spirit. The soul was the first to be deceived and disobeyed. Why are these two points important? Because to the extent that our souls are damaged, our spirit remains undeveloped.

We don't have good receivers in terms of hearing God. Hearing the voice in the wind is an excellent metaphor for hearing the Voice of the Spirit. Get your soul healed – and your whole body will experience a glorious transformation. Disembodied spirits want to manifest, and they need bodies to do that. If they control your body, they access your mind, will, emotions, speech, and actions. Many voices exist in the spirit world. Therefore, whatever is heard must be tested. Does it exalt Jesus Christ? Does it comply with the Scriptures? The answers to these questions help distinguish the voice of God from other agents. *"But solid food is for the mature, for those who have their powers of discernment trained by constant practice to distinguish good from evil."* (Hebrews 5:14)

To clarify, hearing God begins where you are and then progressively moves you toward maturity through many exercises. Our bodies are the temple of God where the Holy Spirit lives. Our bodies can manifest the will of God, the presence of God, and the power of God. When carrying His word, purpose, power, and authority, we have dominion over all things. It becomes the place where the voice of the Father and the son are the same. If we hone our spirit into maturity and desires into godliness, it becomes the filter that every response to life situations passes through. Maturity includes discernment and is true of the opposite. If we allow our souls to rule, we will manifest all the desires and actions of our carnal nature and sink into depravity. Want to know why so many are failing today? They are not discerning! Their filters have not been replaced in a long time.

Long ago, my wife and I moved into a house where the air conditioning filter had not been changed in at least two years. I don't know how the A/C unit kept running. The filter was so thick with dust I could not see through it. As I pulled out the filter, one half inch thick chunks of dust fell on the garage floor. In effect, the air handler could not breathe due to neglect by the previous owner. The clogged filter made the machine work harder, increasing the power bill. Once the maintenance was complete, the air was cleaner, and we all could breathe easier including the machine. It was troubling to witness neglect of something so important.

Sadly today, many Christians have allowed the nature of the soul to dominate their desires. Their filters have not been washed or changed in a very long time. They call it freedom. Their voices echo, "Have freedom, don't be so dull and religious." Freedom is not the same as looseness or neglect. By keeping the filters of our soul clean, we can breathe easier and have less restriction of the spirits flow. We will find the presence of God flowing out of us so that we are able to effectively change the environments around us. Everyone in the room will benefit from the light, joy and freshness of the spirit we walk in.

Accessing Your Spiritual DNA

Your body carries DNA, both spiritual and physical. Other entities (disembodied spirits) want to inhabit your DNA. If they can access your DNA, they have access to your nervous system. Your nervous system is the electrical system of your body. If they access your nervous system, they spread like a computer virus. They have access to your mind, will, and emotions. (the soul realm). If you've ever witnessed a deliverance session, the person being delivered sometimes flips, screams, and flails all over the place. Something else has taken over the mind, will, and emotions that is being driven out.

The DNA in the blood cells carries a code hardwired to your body, mind, and soul. This code carries the properties and nature of reproduction. The code in the DNA determines who you are and how you look. Similarly, as a believer, you are created in the Father's spiritual image and carry His DNA in your spirit. Your spirit reproduces His seed and kind, His nature and kingdom. If other beings can access your spiritual DNA, they produce their kind of fruit, causing you to replicate the unrighteous seed of the enemy. They cause sickness, possession, bondage, dependency, fear, and corruption of every kind.

Daniel Interprets a Dream

In Daniel chapter 2, King Nebuchadnezzar has a dream. Its impact on him was so distressing that he immediately sought an interpretation from his wise men. Even though he couldn't recall any details, he wanted his wise men to tell him the dream and interpret it. Suppose they didn't, then it was off with their head. Wouldn't you agree that's a pretty tough final exam for the first School of Dream Interpretation? Daniel's contemporaries, the other secular wise men, didn't know where to start because they lacked a description of the dream. In frustrated fury, Nebuchadnezzar instructed his bodyguard captain to personally oversee slaughtering the known wise men in his kingdom, including those among the children of Israel, if they failed to interpret the dream. That is never a great idea, killing all the most intelligent people in your kingdom. The enemy is rather dim-witted, isn't he?

Daniel boldly says, "Time out!" He asks the king for time to seek God. "Then Daniel discovers a secret in a night vision," and he blessed God by saying, *He gives wisdom to the wise and knowledge to those who have understanding and reveals deep and secret things; He knows what is in the darkness, and light dwells with Him."* (Dan. 2:19,21-22 NKJV) Instructed by God, Daniel could tell the king exactly what he had dreamed and then interpret it. The secret of dream interpretation is always: to seek God first. *"Trust in the Lord with all your heart, and do not lean on your own understanding. In all your ways acknowledge him, and he will make straight your paths."* (Proverbs 3:5–6) Daniel had a spotless and clear filter to do this. He needed to know what to filter out. His life depended on it at this moment. In these last days, our life will depend on hearing God with clear filters in the realm of Spirit. We need to understand this.

The dream of the king described in Daniel 2 concerned a statue. It was built in successive metal sections from the head to the feet. The five sections represented five historical world powers, beginning with the Babylonian Empire as the head of gold and finishing with the feet and toes of iron mixed with clay. Most scholars agree that the three sections following Babylon represent the Persian, the Greek, and the Roman Empires. However, the identity of the last, the iron mixed with clay, has divided the experts.

The Mystery of Iron and Clay

They can only agree that it represents an end-time power, kingdom, or government destroyed at the coming of God's kingdom. In the dream, "the stone not made with hands" comes from above and utterly smashes the feet of this statue, revealing how the Kingdom of God will deal with this last world power and the kingdom of Satan.

First, we look at the iron and clay mixture. Iron is a manufactured material, representing machinery typical of the Roman Empire and warfare machine, crushing all resistance and overtaking the known world. We know from the Genesis record that God created man from the dust or clay of the earth, so metaphorically and biblically, clay represents humanity. Daniel prophesied these words, "As the toes of the feet were partly of iron and partly of clay, so the last worldly kingdom shall be partly strong and partly fragile." As we saw, iron mixed with clay, *they will mingle with the seed of men; but they will not adhere to one another, just as iron does not mix with clay."* (Daniel 2:42-43) Ceramic clay and iron do not adhere well together. Weakness is introduced into this kingdom, so this empire does not last as a world order. This prophecy passes over the present age and refers to the Revived Roman Empire found in the last generation before Jesus appears back on the scene. The ten toes of the statue relate to the ten-nation confederacy of the Roman Empire in the last days. This is the final formation of the Roman Empire. Many nations and some western powers will be subservient to this ten-nation confederacy. It will permeate both the natural and the spiritual realms.

The phrase "seed of men" implies a grassroots issue; it permeates the masses. Throughout the stream of the Roman Empire, the two issues of monarchy and democracy struggle at the grassroots level. Domestic strife weakens the government so that it cannot reach its objectives. This sets the stage for the final Kingdom. The culmination of Satan's hatred for God and humanity will result in a desire to corrupt the bloodlines, the pure DNA. It foretells a kingdom that combines manufactured machinery (computers) and humans artificially manipulated with technology. A combination of human DNA and machinery, i.e., clay and iron, is also suggested by the multi-headed and horned beast in Revelation 13. *"I saw one of the beast's heads as if it had been mortally wounded, and his deadly wound was healed. All the world marveled and followed the beast."* (Rev. 13:3) One interpretation of this passage in Revelation is a vivid picture of how a machine may be attacked and damaged so that it seems non-functioning. But then it can be repaired to work as well as new. In the same way, a life-like robotic head may appear to have been given a deadly wound but is then miraculously "healed."

I ran across a strange adaptation of clay and iron mixture during my research. Research and technology are advancing at warp speed. There was a research project in 2018 funded by DARPA, the Defense Advanced Research Projects Agency, that demonstrated that a person with a chip embedded in their brain could pilot a swarm of drones using signals from their brain.[xv]

Recently, a research team from Columbia University tested the convergence of neural networks. They combined brain implants, artificial intelligence, and a speech synthesizer to translate brain activity into recognizable robotic words. The implications of this technology are mind-boggling, including allowing paralyzed people the ability to communicate and the potential to read human thoughts via cognitive imaging. To follow this, the Kingdom of Saudi Arabia is reinventing itself as a global pioneer in Industry 4.0. Industry 4.0 is for leveraging Artificial Intelligence to create a fully sustainable and digitally driven future of manufacturing. You can only imagine where that will lead.

American journalist, Kenneth Cukier, reported in a journal put out by the Bank of Argentina, the second-largest in Spain that "upheavals in the Industrial Revolution created political revolutions and gave rise to entirely new economic philosophies and political movements like Marxism. It is not too much of an intellectual stretch to predict that new political philosophies and social movements built up around Big Data, robots, computers, and the internet and their effect on the economy and representation in our democracy today."[xvi]

We are already in the age of the "beast" or, possibly better known as the supercomputer. It's already here. Multiple computer storage banks are currently being built in remote locations so large each one fills a city block. They are building storage systems in places so remote, so uninhabitable to humans, that you have to take a helicopter to get there. These places not only store data for banks and Crypto currencies, but far more. Every conversation, transaction, call, speech, and movement you make is tracked, watched, and recorded.

God Is in Control

God has everything under control. Jesus is the first and the last, the Alpha and Omega, the beginning and the end. Let me remind you that there is no end for the believer. It will be the end of those who oppose Christ. People who look for the miraculous anywhere apart from Jesus Christ will be eager to worship such a beast. They will be deceived and led down the path of the antichrist. Revelation 13 describes the last days' scenario: *"So, they worshiped the dragon who gave authority to the beast, and they worshiped the beast, saying, 'Who is like the beast? Who is able to make war with him?' And he was given a mouth speaking great things and blasphemies, and he was given authority to continue for forty-two months. Then he opened his mouth in blasphemy against God, to blaspheme His name, His tabernacle, and those who dwell in heaven. Authority was given to him over every tribe, tongue, and nation. All who dwell on the earth will worship him, whose names have not been written in the Book of Life of the Lamb slain from the foundation of the world."* (Revelation 13:4-8) He was granted to make war with the saints and overcome them.

Could it be possible that this kingdom of technology, the ultimate expression of anti-Christ, could find a representation in a modern combination of human and synthetic DNA in a false religion of hate that overtakes the world? I do not say this to bring fear but to remind us that when the saints come together to pray in agreement, God puts His finger on the pause button and brings about a reprieve. God did this for Abraham regarding Lot and Sodom. He did it at the tower of Babel. Many believe that during World War 2, the rescue of thousands of soldiers at Dunkirk was a "pause button" in answer to the intercession led by Rees Howell.[xvii]

I want to see the souls in the body of Christ healed and freshly inspired to be in one accord. I want to see them shutting down this anti-Christ spirit by the power of the believers. We can at least put it on hold. God's plan is for us to see the darkness overcome by increasing great light. I believe we can pray and intercede for this process of takeover to be contained so that the world will experience the most remarkable revival it has ever seen. God's heart has always been for a worldwide tsunami of salvations from all tribes and nations. The many little side trips I introduce in these chapters is with the intention of recognizing the significance of hearing the right voice and hearing it distinctly.

The Bible writes about the falling away from hearing the wrong voices in the last days. *"Now the Spirit expressly says that in later times some will depart from the faith by devoting themselves to deceitful spirits and teachings of demons."* (1 Timothy 4:1, ESV) The Bible provides many examples of the spirit/soul crossover phenomenon. The life of King Saul is a classic. In 1 Samuel 10:9-11, Saul was once anointed of God, but Saul allowed himself to be dragged into a life of bitterness, jealousy, unforgiveness, and vengeance due to disobedience and rebellion. An evil spirit affected his physical life and permeated his spiritual walk with God.

Since the gifts of God are irrevocable, it is not uncommon for gifted people who do not know the Lord to stray into the domain of evil power and still show evidence of giftedness. Many gifted people have unknowingly become corrupted. Rather than receiving revelation from God, they operate in familiar spirits. Many New Agers have gifts from God but have crossed over to power on the dark side without knowing it.

When our souls are damaged, our spirits remain undeveloped, and we no longer have excellent "receivers" for hearing God. Think of a small transistor radio with a crackling speaker, making a tinny noise. Compare that to a Bose stereo system today, giving off the full range of symphonic sound. Both receive the same invisible radio waves, but the receiver's quality is vastly more impacting than the transistor radio. Have you ever received a notice on your laptop, "file corrupted, unable to open?" That's what happens to the soul when its filter is damaged. If the soul is not healed and sealed with the blood of Jesus, it remains open for other things to enter. The corrupted file in the soul gets in the way of the pure transmission of the voice.

The Father is not looking for enslaved people and robots. He is looking for voluntary lovers and a pure DNA family who freely surrenders their mind, body, and spirit to His will and makes decisions based on His love. He's not looking for a mixture. The enemy's kingdom is always one of force, coercion, bending your will, stealing your freedom, shutdown, control, etc. In the Kingdom of God, through you make a free-will decision to be like Him, cooperating with heaven, receiving His goodwill nature, and then, together as a family, we restore creation to original intent. Something earthshaking happens when we recognize the voice in the wind. The word of the Lord is alive with creative ability and divine power. As mature sons, when we hear or see in the spirit realm, it may seem that we are receiving information and revelation for the first time. However, I believe the word of the Lord hovers in the atmosphere until we discover and apply what already exists.

Finally, I am reminded of the words in Isaiah 55:11, *"…so is my word that goes out from my mouth: It will not return to me empty but will accomplish what I desire and achieve the purpose for which I sent it."* Mature sons hear the voice, align their hearts with God's Word, and declare it over the earth. When that word is released, it has a supernatural power to change conditions, circumstances, and environments that ultimately shift nations. Nothing changes by itself without the necessary adjustments. But with the correct identity, alignment, and purpose, we will effectively bring about the change as God's representatives on the earth. Amen!

THE END

ENDNOTES

Chapter One
i https://deforestlondon.wordpress.com/2020/03/14/listen-to-the-wind-with-nicodemus (Accessed July 29, 2022).

Chapter Two
ii https://dana.org/article/the-senses-hearing/.com (Accessed July 29, 2022)
iii https://www.desiringgod.org/articles/why-jesus-needed-the-holy-spirit (Accessed Jan 27, 2023)

Chapter Four
iv http://www.esalq.usp.br/lepse/imgs/conteudo_thumb/The-Illusion-of-Reality.pdf (Accessed July 29, 2022)
v https://playbook.noulab.org/mental-models/breath-pattern-divergence-emergence-convergence (Accessed April 23, 2022).
vi https://www.ihopkc.org/resources/books/seven-longings-human-heart/ (Accessed April 23, 2022).

Chapter Six
vii https://pdfcoffee.com/celtic-flame-pdf-free.html (Accessed May 20, 2022).
viii https://ajrca.edu/parsha/parshat-tzav-2/ (Accessed May 20, 2022).
ix https://skipmoen.com/2010/02/where-is-it-2/ (Accessed May 20, 2022).

Chapter Seven
x https://www.biblestudytools.com/dictionaries/bakers-evangelical-dictionary/time.html (Accessed July 27, 2022)

Chapter Eleven
xi https://www.biblestudytools.com/lexicons/hebrew/nas/elohiym.html (Accessed June 10, 2022).

Chapter Twelve
xii https://www.biblestudytools.com/lexicons/greek/nas/anakrino.html (Accessed July 1, 2022).

xiii https://biblestudylessons.net/Comics/Greek%20to%20me/psyche.html (Accessed July 2, 2022).
xiv https://www.biblestudytools.com/lexicons/greek/nas/amemptos.html (Accessed July 3, 2022).
xv https://www.darpa.mil/news-events/2019-05-20
xvi https://www.bbvaopenmind.com/wp-content/uploads/2015/02/BBVA-OpenMind-book-Reinventing-the-Company-in-the-Digital-Age-business-innovation1.pdf (Accessed July 3, 2022).
xvii https://soulpants.wordpress.com/2008/02/11/reese-howells-writes (Accessed July3, 2022)

ABOUT THE AUTHOR

Whether dirt biking in South Africa, hiking the Swiss Alps, exploring pyramids in Egypt, camping on top of Mt. Sinai, climbing a volcano in Guatemala, or trekking inside the Arctic Circle, David L. Ramer has always had a passion for adventure. Coming from a long generational line of Hebrew and Bible scholars, pastors, teachers and church planters traced nearly back to the Reformation, David followed his heart traveling and ministering in 38 nations. His ministry adventures include the extremes of the back roads of Mexico and Brazil, visiting a leper colony in India, an end-of-the-road Zulu school in South Africa, and Inuit villages in Alaska and more. His educational trips include visiting art museums, countless biblical and historical sites in Israel, Europe, Asia, and the Middle East.

After exploring the world, David settled in and earned his Master of Divinity degree from Tabernacle Bible College and Seminary. For the past fifteen years, he and his wife, Ronda, have founded and pastored Glory Fire Church in Lake Mary, FL, a regional apostolic training and equipping center with a vision to reach nations. Together, they have spent years travelling the globe with a recent focus on South Korea. David is an admired prophetic teacher with a consistent ability to bring supernatural revelation and impartation, giving the Body of Christ an understanding of their true identity as sons.

Besides writing, his other passions include music and art where after just three years of painting, his art is collected in three nations and viewed worldwide. Some of his artwork can be found on his website at www.davidramerart.com. He lives in Central Florida with his wife and their beloved little wire-hair fox terrier named Hootie, who is well known and loved by friends on 5 continents. From here, the journey continues in his books.

www.ingramcontent.com/pod-product-compliance
Lightning Source LLC
Chambersburg PA
CBHW040141160726
48006CB00014B/1579